The author at Grand Canyon National Park, Arizona.

LIVING LARGE IN NATURE

LIVING LARGE IN NATURE

A WRITER'S IDEA OF CREATIONISM

BY REG SANER

Center Books in Natural History
George F. Thompson, series founder and director

THE CENTER FOR AMERICAN PLACES
at Columbia College Chicago

Copyright © 2010 The Center for American Places at Columbia College Chicago.
Photographs © 2010 Reg Saner, except for the frontispiece: © 2010 Ron Billingsley.
All rights reserved.
Published 2010. First Edition.
Printed in the United States of America on acid-free paper.

The Center for American Places at Columbia College Chicago
600 South Michigan Avenue
Chicago, Illinois 60605–1996, U.S.A.
www.americanplaces.org

Distributed by the University of Chicago Press
www.press.uchicago.edu

18 17 16 15 14 13 12 11 10   1 2 3 4 5

Library of Congress Cataloging-in-Publication Data
Saner, Reg.
  Living large in nature : a writer's idea of creationism / by Reg Saner. — 1st edition.
        p. cm. —   (Center books in natural history ; 4)
  Includes bibliographical references.
  ISBN: 978–1–935195–08–5 (alk. paper)
  1. Creationism. 2. Nature. I. Title. II. Series.

  BS660.S26 2010
  231.7'652—dc22

2009053507

For Jane Bock,
bio-savant
and large-hearted begetter
of this little book

Felix, qui potuit rerum cognoscere causas . . .
—Virgil, *Georgics,* II

CONTENTS

PROLOGUE

IN COMPARING a closed world with an open one, *Living Large in Nature* illustrates an aspect of religion's uneasy relation to science through the example of Creationism. It does so because young-Earth Creationism—and its thinly disguised second coming as Intelligent Design—offer conspicuous instances of humanity's peculiar ability to believe the unbelievable. More seriously, they exemplify the sort of dogma-bound vision which sees an enemy in true science and all who disagree. From there it's but a short step to squadrons of Thought Police and far worse. And, in that spirit, the kinship between religious zealots and political ideologies is still striking both in the United States and abroad.

Because my two greatest delights are language and the natural world—as I hope will become apparent in the following pages—I admire Charles Darwin (1809–1882) both for his role in bringing coherence to our understanding of ourselves and all life-forms and for his written mastery of the English tongue.[1] I am, therefore, offended by those who blacken his name in the name of religion. They fear science for its openness to new knowledge, whereas their dogmas bind them to denial instead of discovery.

This book does not, however, attempt a biologically detailed critique of Creationism. By now an impressive number of excellent publications offer such analyses. Instead, the paradoxical resort by its spokesmen (invariably male) to immoral behavior in the name of morality seems far more interesting. Then, too, because my personal way of being and seeing is incorrigibly religious, I find in Creationism's antipathy to science a perversion of the religious spirit.

Readers who feel little interest in fundamentalist cults naturally assume that hardly anyone these days takes Creationism seriously.[2] Nonetheless, its campaign to undermine biological science and impose its sectarian faith on science education in schools and universities is ominously well organized and well funded. My touching only briefly on the movement's ultimate goal of ending the separation between church and state doesn't mean I take the threat lightly.

Throughout these pages, by way of making a crucial distinction, references to my sort of lower-case creationism won't be capitalized, whereas all mention of Genesis-inspired Creationism and its disguise as Intelligent Design, or ID, will be so denoted, just as we capitalize the names of any sect.

Finally, because my kind of creationism entails a mode of self-organizing, which is to say self-evolving through writing, I have—by way of illustration—necessarily drawn on many passages which first appeared in one or another of my previous three books of nonfiction. Rather than distort or dilute them to paraphrased versions, I've sometimes retained their original wording. I also wish to thank the following publications in which parts of this book first appeared: *Ecotone, The Georgia Review, The Gettysburg Review, The Quarterly Review of Literature,* and *The Writer's Chronicle.*

The author's son, Nick, hiking the high country of Colorado's Indian Peaks Wilderness Area.

Alpine buttercups (*Ranunculus adoneus*) in Colorado's Indian Peaks Wilderness Area.

Fern Creek, along the Odessa Lake trail in Rocky Mountain National Park, Colorado.

Gateway Arch in Arches National Park, Utah.

A CHALLENGE

CAN YOU IMAGINE anything more strange? I cannot. Taken alive by a cosmos! As that situation has slowly dawned on me, I've become rich in unanswered questions. But, then, who in only a lifetime can expect to unriddle the world?

Even so, I like being cosmic. I find it peculiar but flattering. Having given our universe the best years of my life, I do wish it weren't so aloof. I wish it would take more of an interest. I wish I knew what its plans are. "Okay," I say to it, "you exist, I exist. So where does that leave us? And why must I do all the talking?"

The oddity of being alive in a place called "the world" does that to a person. From a sidereal perspective, living matter embodies "a highly improbable state." So, considering all the inanimate matter in the universe, "alive" is hyper-highly abnormal. But why? Good question.

Speaking of questions, sooner or later doesn't every child ask, "Mommy, where did I come from?" These days, however, with low-rider jeans, mothers dressing their ten-year-old daughters like French tarts, boy/girl dialogues of single entendre, and teens copulating as if humans were an endangered species, no parent could invoke the stork and keep a straight face. Is there one mother left who tells her child, "Why, sweetie pie, we found you under a cabbage leaf."

Way back in the psychedelic sixties, my friend Jo Ann said nothing of the kind. For her five-year old Chris she went into physiologic details. She didn't just refer vaguely to "certain body parts." She named names. His eyes widened. She implicated his father. Said that she and he had been in cahoots on it. The boy was stunned, aghast, revolted. These were people he had respected. The very people who kept telling him to behave himself. Then, remembering he had a younger sister, he cried out in dismay, "You don't mean you did it *twice?*"

If ever there were a "fall into knowledge," it's that one. It changes the child by putting him further into the real than he had dreamed or wanted to be—a strange new context of animality. Small wonder that many children, perhaps most, prefer not to think of their parents as sex mates.

There are plenty of other things we adults don't like to ponder. For example, the size of all we belong to and the pitiful brevity of our visit. Post-Darwin, our biological status is another aspect some among us would rather not dwell on. Like little Chris, surprising numbers of adults convinced of Creationism in its guise as Intelligent Design vehemently deny their double nature as fur-bearing critters with vestigial claws on hands and feet; animals who talk and think, yet who, like our mammalian kin, also copulate and give suck. In a nutshell, Creationists simply can't stand the facts of life. That's why they throw hissy fits.

Despite our high-tech culture, pollsters consistently tell us a majority of the U.S. population don't believe they evolved. In a Harris poll of June 2005, sixty-four percent of the respondents said humans were created directly by God.

Hello? Entire libraries of scientific evidence globally agreed upon as valid now testify to the *fact* of evolution as well as to the fact that this universe and world are wildly peculiar beyond knowing. Yet, in 2006, *Science* magazine published results of an even wider, if earlier survey, which showed that, out of thirty-four industrialized nations, only Turkey ranks lower than the U.S. in public acceptance of evolution.[1] Shown the statement "Human beings, as we know them, developed from earlier species of animals," those polled were asked if that were true or false. In the U.S. only, forty percent said "True," whereas in Catholic Ireland more than sixty percent thought it valid.

A preference for evidence of what's truest, soothing or not, explains why a few years ago I accepted an invitation to debate a Creationist. My university colleague and friend Jane Bock, a distinguished biologist, had been the initial recipient of that invitation. She and other biologists often receive such challenges but routinely ignore them as a waste of time. Then, looking at me, Jane's mischievous streak kicked in. "How about you?" she said, knowing of my intense admiration for Darwin. "Do you want to take them on?"

Never in my adult life had I encountered a Creationist. Now here was an opportunity to practice my favorite occupation: going forth to see for myself. I said, "Okay, I'll do it." Why? Well, fools do rush in.

True, as an English teacher I was hardly a Creationist's ideal target. Their spokesmen hope to worst some biologically competent foe whose defeat would "send a message." But, as a mere ink-stained wretch from an English Department, I had the merit of being a sitting duck. Blowing me away would reveal what sort of lightweight chumps follow the abominable Darwin, the nemesis whose very name still causes some pillars of the Religious Right to go rigid and show only the whites of their eyes.

Although once a passionate Creationist myself, I had forgotten that phase of my life. Mistakenly thinking I'd never laid eyes on such a living fossil—although our so-called modern world teems with them—I accepted the challenge in Jane's stead and looked forward to a lively time. Oh, I knew well enough that hard-line Creationists have become such a target as to be shunned by even their spun-off counterparts, the proponents of Intelligent Design.

That very fact made me all the keener to lay eyes on an old-style Creationist before the breed went extinct. Also, because one of my culture heroes is Darwin, their slanders of him and evolution bug me. Take, for instance, these typical slurs found in the preface to a high-school textbook written explicitly for confuting Darwinians:

> Historically, biology was the first major area of assault in the American classroom as evolution permeated the schools in the 1920's. Even today, evolutionism poisons biology textbooks and distracts from God's glory in creation. . . . Evolution is presented for what it is—a retreat from science.

Students and teachers alike will feel more comfortable when they realize that it is not biology that is in conflict with Scripture, but rather the ungodly philosophy of some biologists.[2]

Evolution poisons? Promulgating such ignorance is bad enough in itself, yet Earth's health is also at stake. Recently, the science academies of sixty-seven countries published a statement decrying such anti-intellectualism. Among other things it made this vital point: *"Knowledge of the natural world in which they live empowers people to meet human needs and protect the planet"* (my emphasis).[3] Might I possibly open a mind or two?

Our debate was to be held at the Bethany Baptist Church suburb of Aurora before a mostly "saved" congregation in which Creationist doctrine is simply the truth. Although I myself had once been of their opinion on that topic, I'd momentarily forgotten that phase of my religious history.

At what age I let myself be gathered to the bosom of Creationism I can't recall, yet it must have happened by the time I was five and in first grade. My memory of just how it happened remains clear as the image of tall Sister Mary Daniel in her great black wimple and Dominican habit of ankle-length white linen, as she tested us first-graders with the very first question in the *Baltimore Catechism,* "Who made us?"

On cue, we chirruped like a classroom of sparrows, "God made us."

To say Sister did the asking and we the believing would, however, be quite false. Belief implies the possibility of disbelief, a thing literally unthinkable at that age. Children may be finicky eaters, yet, when it comes to religion, they down whatever's set before them. If your parents follow Jainism, you follow them. Besides, anything Sister Mary Daniel said was true.

How, you may ask, could a five-year-old know that?

It wasn't so much that she wore holy clothes covering all but her face and hands nor that all the mothers, including mine, spoke to her as to a Very Special Person. It wasn't even because she always seemed so clean and gave off such a nice, soapy fragrance. What Sister Mary Daniel said was true because she was tall, patient, soft-spoken, and kind to every one of us children.

I see her yet, standing at the front of the room, the polished beads of her long Dominican rosary dangling from a black-leather belt round her waist. With her right hand, she holds up a level row of yellow shapes stuck to a red stick: 0 1 2 3 4 5 6 7 8 9; with the other, she points to each shape in turn and gives it a name, which we all repeat aloud. Katie Stanley and Edmund Ferry had gone to kindergarten and already knew their numbers. They were our class's intellectuals, whereas I found that Sister's remarks cleared up much puzzlement over those shapes. What's more, I've drawn on the information ever since.

Not only my arithmetical education began with Sister Mary Daniel. So did my literary training. She moved among our desks, hovering, observing, suggesting, while our young fingers tried to wrest from a cheap pencil that parade of odd shapes called the alphabet. To this day, if when in writing my name I give a nice fat curve to its first capital, I imagine her saying, "That's a good R, Reginald." (My father was a Reginald, which explains how my life came to be blighted at the font.) I sometimes smile to find myself carefully forming its cursives, as if hoping for Sister's nod of approval. Many are the ways to be a good teacher, a good pupil. The best of them is love. Was she pretty? I don't remember, just that she was beautiful.

Surprising as it should have been to learn I'd been made by God, it never entered my noodle to ask why. It just seemed to be what God does. He makes things. Unlike the grown-up kind of Creationist, I didn't at the least mention of Darwin grind my teeth and spit. I was proud of my spitting, but hadn't yet heard of evolution, so there was no need for righteous saliva. All the same, as we children grew older we did learn that a hellish fate awaits that soul guilty of willfully doubting things the *Baltimore Catechism* says are eternally true, and its pages clearly give top billing to the Creator.

I certainly got plenty of that catechism. Its current edition runs to 352 pages, but each of us children had a mercifully downsized and simplified version from which to memorize Q&A sections. In theory, it offered divine knowledge as revealed by God, but all through grade school we called it homework. The unabridged edition, for example, follows "Who made us?" with further explanation, using lots of big words way over young heads. Yet its logic would have drawn hallelujahs from the most hard-shell Creationist:

"Reason unaided by revelation can prove that God exists. It knows that this vast universe could not have come into being by its own powers. The movement of creatures and their dependence upon one another, the various degrees of perfection found in them, the fact that they come into being and cease to be, and, finally, the marvelous order in the universe, demand the existence of an almighty power and the wisdom of an eternal intelligent cause that we call God."[4]

No taint of diabolical Darwinism there, merely a recurrence of the someone-must-have-done-this argument, discussed below in "William Paley's Very Wonderful Watch." (Always some *one*, never some *thing*.) By high school, however, Father O'Connor—a tall, dark-haired, and handsome man who cut quite a dashing figure in our parish—told us the Church doesn't condemn evolution. Not so long as we realize that somewhere in the process God added an immortal soul to all the humans descended from primates. At football practice our coach sometimes claimed we were descended from jellyfish, but he didn't offer it as a scientific proposition.

Having cited a passage from the catechism's edition for high-schoolers and grownups, I should now add another which wasn't in our grade school copies. It occurs in Lesson 5, "The Creation and the Fall of Man," which comments on God's creating Adam and Eve: "The theory of evolution . . . has offered no convincing scientific proof that the human body developed gradually from that of a lower animal."[5] This remark was printed with Church approval, despite more than a century of scientific evidence amassed all over the world in circumstantial support of our primate ancestry. As for "convincing scientific proof," there is none whatever for either *The Holy Bible*'s claim or the Church's claim to divine authority.[6]

Yes, evidence of our animal origin does lack eyewitnesses. In contrast, teachers of chemistry can easily *prove* that steel wool burns furiously in an atmosphere of pure oxygen. To a classroom of pupils they simply show it happening. Bioscientists are bone weary, however, of having to remind anti-Darwinians that our animal origin can't be *proven*, owing to the fact that not only was there no one to see it happen, but it could not have been seen—even by a blue-ribbon panel of observers. The transition from a precursor species to our own would have been so gradual that no distinct line can be drawn between them. As far as that goes, the divine creation of every creeping thing along with Adam and Eve had no eye-witnesses either.

In the *Baltimore Catechism No. 3*, a further reference to evolution occurs several pages later, admitting, "God could have brought the human race into existence in this way," then insists on God nonetheless endowing each human with an immortal soul.[7] We children also learned that a hellish fate awaits that soul guilty of willfully doubting what the *Baltimore Catechism* says are the eternal verities in the matter.

Me disagree with the catechism? Only heretics did that. Even if I didn't quite know what a heretic was, I did know it was the baddest thing you could become. Maybe the word's sound caused me to picture a hairy man in grubby clothes; a swarthy, red-eyed man who stood glaring at me and who, without lifting a finger, was unspeakably wicked.

A despondent lass in an old play says, "We know what we are but know not what we may be." Well, the skinny little blue-eyed kid I once was is now himself a full-grown, double-damned heretic—though not particularly hairy. And how, you may ask, did that happen? It happened the day I awoke to the one fact of life that makes all the others inexhaustibly fascinating: the fact that nobody knows what this world is or why.

In a letter to the program director of the Bethany Evangelical Church of Aurora, I explained that Professor Jane Bock had suggested I accept its debate invitation in her stead. His reply naturally asked about my qualifications. My answer referred him to literary essays I had written in which Darwin and the geological age of Earth were main themes. I soon received another letter, one unexceptionably courteous and detailed, sketching the debate's procedure. It also informed me that my opponent would be a Mr. Binford Pyle, who—as I learned from the Internet—was a maker of Creationist videos and a faculty member in something called the Farview Academy, a camp for educating young Creationists. My upbringing had given me firsthand experience with the closed mind. After all, I used to have one.

As a devout boy I was moved by the polychrome beauty of Catholic belief, with its altars, pious statues, gold-plated tabernacle and chalices; a boy who revered the priest's sacred mumble, his colorful vestments, the lit candles, incense, and choral voices backed by organ chords; a boy who enjoyed the warmth of our congregation's unanimous murmurs in response to mass Latin. For two or three years I even imagined I had a priestly calling. Finally, though, what Holy Mother Church calls "our God-given power to reason" sent me in the opposite direction.

Having been taught that life beyond the grave will be vast as eternity, I must admit not even the American West confers that kind of size. All the same, the West, along with evolutionary science and astronomy, offers an immediate way of living large, as I'll explain.

BORN AGAIN

MY POET-FRIEND Wayne once asked why, out of all the poetry I'd written, almost none drew on my native Midwest. By way of answer, I could only shrug and say, "Beats me."

"It can't be true," I later scolded myself, "that my life began in Colorado." By then, hadn't I finished college? Hadn't I seen parts of Asia? Hadn't I led an infantry platoon in combat? Hadn't I studied in Europe?

So it can't be true. What's more—seeing peoples and places of the Far East, ducking from snipers and shellfire, gawking at ruins in the Roman Forum, cruising the waterways of Venice, wandering among the frescoed ceilings and *palazzi* of Florence—each left indelible memories. Yet only in the American West have I felt born again—body, mind, and soul—a birthing fused with the writing its forests and mountains and meadows begot. To claim the West superior to the Midwest, the East, or, for that matter, Madagascar is silly. The West is simply better for me, a Big Picture person by nature, who is happier out-of-doors than within.

A particular ski trip in January in the Colorado Rockies illustrates what I mean, but, first, there is the story of how I wasn't paying attention when I got born the first time and blew it.

⁜

In fairness to my Illinois hometown of Jacksonville, 230 level miles south of Chicago, I must say I shared the local pride in our summer-rich acres of Illinois corn, soybeans, wheat, and cattle, a pride sprung from the fertility of our Morgan County soil. But man does not live by grain alone.

If in damp weather you wanted to stretch your legs, you could stroll over either sidewalk or soil which, even in wooded areas, could be muddy enough to ball up quickly and cling to your boot soles like leg weights. Besides, almost all acreage surrounding our town was either under cultivation or enriched with cow flop from grazing stock. Public lands? Apart from our nine-hole golf course and park there were none.

More crucially, even on the clearest days, I couldn't see the world from there.

Instead, I saw a landscape of human purpose rationalized by section lines, fences, and furrows. Admirable in its way, of course. Who could be against food? But the great geologic depths and heights, the unimprovable expanses so characteristic of the monumental West I love were nowhere to be seen. Our town's loftiest altitudes were the tees on our nine-hole golf course. Laughably enough, my first descent on real skis, not kid-made versions, took off from lip of the seventh tee. I managed to glide over snow and winter grass some twenty feet before I fell sprawling.

Between working for my dad, playing night baseball, and golfing with five mismatched clubs older than I was, sports helped my adolescence through summer. That and the girls at our Nichols Park swimming pool or dance pavilion. Winters, though, were a total loss. November bleakness over vistas of ploughed furrows induced a subspecies of Arctic melancholia, in a town whose local hot spot was the bowling alley—called, of course, The Bowl Inn. Facing a new morning, you'd squint out the window at gray sky and black elms standing around naked; then, for no reason you could name without being rude to the neighbors, your heart would struggle not to feel like a coal mine.

My immigrant great-grandfather Saner, aged and grown childish, often paced to and fro in front of his son's Illinois house, half-mumbling, half-chanting a longing for his beloved Switzerland. Thus, I've sometimes wondered if his montane genes might not have been restlessly stirring in me as I sat daydreaming out the school windows, wishing our town had a hill.

Jacksonville's worthy thousands, who enjoyed our pleasant community in wise contentment, could certainly have set me straight: "This here's a right fine place; it's you that's the problem." Oh, how truly they'd have spoken! Those good people should have booted me into exile wearing a T-shirt, silk-screened at public expense: INGRATE & MISFIT!

In India, don't untouchables tinkle a little bell so as to warn others they are coming?

That January outing mentioned earlier began at a high-country trailhead. As snowfall deepened the perfect absence of sound, I checked the tiny Weather Bob thermometer on my pack. Three below zero. Then stepped onto my skis and headed up toward a hut just below the Western Continental Divide, with my whispery, cross-country stride taking me past tall Douglas-fir and Engelmann spruce. Each bough was so laden with snow the entire forest felt like a held breath. Sometimes my poles sank two feet without hitting rock. And more snow was coming down.

Lest I sound like some barrel-chested he-man, let me be frank. My style as a backcountry skier is more prose than poetry, but I get around well enough for my purpose.

As an erstwhile Midwesterner, just to be in the Rockies' winter terrain keeps me in ongoing amazement. Absolutely nothing's more beautiful than a snow-covered forest, though daylight beauty wasn't my sole purpose. Higher on Guinn Mountain sits a small cabin mostly hidden by trees, a structure everyone calls "the Arestua hut," so named by Ingvar Sodol. As a Scandinavian who helped build it, he tells me it means "smoke house." It was there I planned to overnight and maybe do some moonlight skiing a bit higher yet, atop the Divide.

Near 10,000 feet I reached a modest headwall, one where I've always told my-self, "Now for the hard part." To one side and just below its rise sag the dregs of a miner's cabin whose collapsed timbers have often been my lunch site. This time, however, a late start put me there near dusk, pausing to assess the snow before start-ing the laborious side-stepping upward. Between altitude and packweight—sleeping bag, water, food, pint of red wine, extra clothing, ski waxes, ski-repair kit, first-aid stuff, compass, fire starter, flashlight, and two candles—that brief ascent soon had me puffing. With flakes falling through an audible stillness deep as peace, I continued upward to the Divide, the whispery glide of my skis taking me higher and higher. All about me in a visible silence stood tall Douglas-fir and Engelmann spruce heaped with storybook snow.

I was alone, healthy, strong, and—as an erstwhile Midwesterner—amazed just to be there, doing what I was doing. I'd seen no other skier all afternoon. My elderly Volvo wagon was far down the mountain, several steeply winding miles away at the trailhead. Skiing the backcountry alone is generally held to be foolhardy, and I agree. It's unwise and I know it. On the other hand, even a single companion makes any out-ing a partly social experience. Only alone in wilderness can you be completely there, with a whiff of "what if?" dilating the soul.

About 600 feet higher and pausing for breath I noticed—some thirty yards to my left and above me across a treeless ravine—a stand of unusually beautiful spruce ar-rayed like spectators along the ravine's edge. Higher yet on their steep mountainside, other evergreens in the waning light ranged through ghostly gradations of gray, with the forms of trees even higher thinning toward invisibility. Meanwhile, as the flakes kept blurring past my eyelashes, I stood so awestruck by those spruce trees they be-came worthy elders grown wise on ages of mountain weather.

From some primitive level in me a spontaneous reverence emanated across the ravine to their snow-laden selves, beings only a century or two less mortal than me. Despite our differing longevities and our two kinds of breathing, we owed our exis-tence to sunlight, soil, and that most mysterious of elements, water—its veil of six-sided crystals slanting down through the speaking stillness between.

The more I stood looking, the more I felt looked at. The very quiet of their white boughs seemed to imply they knew things. The better to listen, I leaned slightly forward on my skis toward another world, theirs. Out of my life while still in it.

With maybe two miles further to the hut, my ongoing delight helped ease fatigue. Summer mountains with their wildflowers by the tens of thousands are more user-friendly, but winter forest—its audible hush thickened by verticalities like white plumes—so enchants me that, after decades, I'm still unsure which season I prefer. All the while, more flakes slanting soundlessly down induced a matching silence in me.

Overhead the cover of gray cloud was growing dusky. With moonrise around five p.m., even a three-quarter moon wouldn't be much help till higher in the sky—and none at all unless weather cleared, which, with the chill-down of nightfall, it often does.

The Colorado Mountain Club owns the Arestua, but it's always unlocked, so anyone can use it. If you care to, you put a couple of bucks in the donation can, but that's up to you. And, since there's no reservation system, it's "first come, first served." Already it could be sheltering other skiers lounging round the stove, ones who've come up from the other side of the Continental Divide. Or perhaps none. Seeing nobody else all afternoon set me guessing. Was it the cold? My car had been one of only two other vehicles when I parked at the trailhead. In warmer weather, there are often three times as many.

Best case, any skiers already at the hut would have the balky wood stove going strong, which can be a chore. Otherwise, except for wind the cabin is as cold inside as out—and, because the stove's a slow learner, you get no heat to speak of till thirty minutes or so after your first match. That's why I've always covered the last mile hoping somebody's there. Too, in wild weather it's possible to ski right past the hut, then have to backtrack, gropingly. Energy I preferred not to spend.

Nearing thick trees where I knew the cabin just had to be, I grinned broadly in relief. There it indeed was, nearly buried. A full meter of wind-carven snow covered the roof and curled down over the eaves, as if in a Russian folk tale, complete with candle glow coming from the one window. I thought of all the stories featuring lost travelers who spy a light shining through the trees. A hermit's hut, maybe, or a wood-cutter's, or the abode of a kindly old woman secretly evil. At that, the cabin's window and door were only partly visible, the rest overwhelmed by drifts—into which were stuck three pair of skis and their poles.

I thrust my own skis into the same drift, shook snow off my hat, parka, gaiters, and boots so as to track in as little as possible, then opened the door on a candle-lit trio of male faces, their eyes asking, "Who's he?"

Among outdoor types a tacit rapport soon develops in respect for shared passion, as if to say, "You wouldn't be here if you weren't one of us."

Chris, a big man with a coppery beard, claimed he and Larry meant to stay the entire weekend. He'd already fried their steak and onions. Having eaten, the two of them were sipping from steel Sierra cups. Like the other two, the third was in his stocking feet. He interrupted his apple-eating long enough to lean forward and shake my hand, murmuring in a German accent, "I'm Wolfgang." Larry offered me some of their Merlot. I thanked him, saying I'd brought my own.

Chris had just gone through a divorce and missed seeing his little girl in the worst way. Since they were pals from way back, Larry had convinced him that a weekend getaway spent skiing around on Guinn Mountain would help Chris deal with things.

The hut has a few pots and pans, kept clean by the last user on the honor system. I stepped outside with one, scooped up enough snow for my stew, and set it atop the stove, an oblong box of black iron on iron legs. Into the melt water I poured crumbles of ground beef pre-cooked at home, adding miso, chopped green pepper, chopped onion, and two pinches of red chili flakes.

While tending its simmer I learned that Larry, who had a droll sense of humor, worked as a finish-carpenter and that Chris cooked the breakfast and lunch menu for Rocky Mountain Joe's, a popular cafe down in Boulder. Wolfgang, a man of maybe fifty, said he'd come from Austria to Montana when he was twenty-eight. He had grown up skiing in Austria and was currently helping with a NASA project at Ball

Aerospace, also in Boulder. Chris knew some cafe customers who worked at Ball. All the while my stew bubbled, our candles burnt clear, the stove radiated warmth, and the hut's unpainted walls and bunks felt luxurious. Just the other side of the door lay all the powder skiing we could want.

Once I had spooned hot food into myself, I grew perkier. In an invitational tone, said I might ski up to the summit by moonlight. Already we were at about 10,600, with the peak only a couple of hundred feet higher.

Chris took thought, then said, "I'm not so sure I'm into pulling on boots again tonight," but Larry said, "C'mon, you know you'll love it!" Chris grunted and gave in. Smiling, Wolfgang began lacing up, then strapping on gaiters.

Through deep powder, the four of us took turns trail-breaking, slogging single file up through a succession of traverses toward the summit, in night silence broken only by heavy breathing. By then it had dipped to eleven below. Though exertion kept me plenty warm, my face smarted in the steady current of arctic air flowing over the Divide. Driven crystals too fine to see kept up a steady prickle on cheeks and eyelids. I put on my yellow-visored goggles, which helped but quickly fogged, so I stuffed them back into my parka and kept climbing.

The sky had opened enough to give us a peek-a-boo moon waxing and waning as archipelagos of cloud went sliding steadily eastward. Even when the moon was clearest, reading the drifts was pure guesswork. I'd ready myself for what seemed a shallow descent, then abruptly lurch onto a steep upward dune of snow.

Once atop the broad summit we fanned out, each of us a dreamwalker moving in meditatively slo-mo through moonlit powder. From time to time I halted, listening to nothing. Or would peer toward ghost-like mountains a mile across the valley, entranced by how their dark granite kept melting to cloud, then re-materializing, coming forward out of the moonlit gray only to dissolve once more. Fascinated, I myself grew slowly invisible with them, then again visible, a floating echo of their apparitional fade and return.

By skiing down a little way into a stand of subalpine fir and out of the summit's wind chill, I perfected my trancelike state. Unseen beneath that cloud-veiled moon I watched dim figures ski past or heard a random call. An indeterminate word. Then another. Then perfect quiet. Then a muffled yelp. Another shadow's gliding blur would seem motion without shape. When one shadow tumbled and sprawled, I could hear it was Chris in powder so deep no one could get hurt.

They say you can't see color by moonlight, but, whenever its three-quarter orb cleared, fine spindrift crystals glittered the air between us, their sparkle hinting at prism-like colors. I, therefore, stood enthralled, my face smarting with cold yet completely fulfilled by where and what I was in that moment. "Oh yes, this. Right here. Right now."

After all, if taking time to be fully alive isn't creationism, what is? When joy suddenly fuses with awe at realizing you're ever so briefly a part of this fathomless mystery we call the world, I call that moment truly religious.

ECOTONE MADE OF WORDS

Le secret dessein de l'artiste est de se faire autre e plus qu'il est . . . par son oeuvre.[1]
—Paul Valéry, *Cahiers*

THE GREATEST STORY ever told? In truth, that's life's evolution, the long process of self-organization that began, presumably, with the first prokaryotic cells, those without a nucleus. My hypothetical "presumably" recognizes the fact that life's origin isn't known. I can almost hear Creationists cry, "Ha! Hear that? He admits it!" Their doctrinal tendency of claiming a supernatural cause for phenomena which biological science can't yet explain is, of course, a logical fallacy. As the German poet and amateur scientist Goethe dryly reminded his fellows, "Not every mystery is a miracle."

Presumably, too, life's self-organizing principle led to eukaryotic cells, those including a nucleus, and from them more complex organisms followed—over great spans of time—to become the mind-boggling diversity of species now alive in their teeming millions. Contrary to what Creationists allege, conjectures about life's biochemical start don't imply godlessness. A Darwin contemporary, one Charles Kingsley, who was also an Anglican priest, saw God as using evolution to make "things make themselves."[2]

Figuratively speaking, my way of creationism parallels evolution by an analogous sort of self-organization or self-creation. Although writing happens to be my path to that goal, it's only one of many available. Any such path, if seriously followed— whether in science, art, or literature—changes us by becoming part of what we are, thus amounting to a form of self-creation by virtue of making us incrementally more complex. Through the enhanced awareness which results, the self has, to that incremental degree, evolved upward—but only if we allow it to happen.

Being myself a word-person from childhood on, my love of language and what it can do inclined me toward the writing process. So that's the path I'll talk about, simply because mine is the self I know best. Nonetheless, it's a creationism available to anyone who cares to give it a try.

As a sometime leader of writing workshops, I've seen students impress themselves with the self-creation which writing can bring about. I've even seen it change lives. I know. That sounds like something a carnival pitchman would say . . . except that psychotherapists have for years found value in encouraging victims of emotional trauma to write about their experiences and reactions. Yet healing is neither my motive for writing nor is it the reason I might encourage others.

The word "might" is mighty relevant here, because for me to give readers a hard sell in that direction really would turn me into a snake-oil salesman. A path you've been talked into is a path without a heart.

As is true of every endeavor, nothing ventured, nothing gained. Anyone deciding to give this lower-case creationism a try knows you don't play a piano well by just wishing. When it comes to musical instruments, everyone understands that but not when it comes to the instrument called language. The common denominator shared by achievement in music, photography, or quilting is love; but, if that term seems too touchy-feely, call it delight. Has there ever been a good musician indifferent to the various combinations of sound? Or a worthwhile writer unexcited by words?

Speaking of a path with a heart, it's only sensible to ask, "Have I got what it takes?" Happily, the all-time best answer to the question of writing potential is a disarmingly simple remark by Annie Dillard, author of *Pilgrim at Tinker Creek* (1974)

and many other books. After a reading, she stood chatting with young fans and wanna
-be authors when one said, "I've been wondering about becoming a writer myself.
What do you think?"

Dillard's response was perfection itself: "Well . . . do you like sentences?"[3]

Although I failed to see it at the time, my friend Wayne's asking why my poetry never
draws on my Midwestern roots had an obvious answer. With me, the impulse to write
has always begun in a fusion of love and wonder, whereas "prairie terrain"—admirable in a dozen ways—just didn't beget their interactive intensity. Apropos of that mo-
tivation, Plato, in his dialogue titled *Theaetetus,* says, "The sole origin of philosophy is
wonder." I'd say it's also crucial to the origin of religion. Yet it took me an embarrass-
ingly long time to understand that much of my writing, whether verse or prose, has
been—in a sense of the word *very* different from its workaday meaning—religious.
Then, too, life for me is far more a question of place than of people, and mine began
where I didn't belong.

Prior to becoming a Westerner, I had pestered reams of innocent paper with
academic writing, thereby adding to the scholarly flea market which few outside
academe ever rummage among. Producing pages for learned journals felt more like
homework than a path with a heart. Once I faced that mismatch, the wide-open West
drew me to write about terrain I loved like a rebirth.

Admittedly, not everybody is turned on by high granite. While in the Army, I met
a Kansan named Scaggs who hated the Rockies. Having honeymooned amid them he
said, "That was all I needed. I seen enough mountains to last me."

Well, okay. If the lone and largely level plains of Kansas are still giving him joy,
so much the better. Anne and I honeymooned in the same mountains and felt just the
opposite. There you see plutonic rock risen from molten depths of the planet, ocean
bottoms thrust up to be summits. Below their tremendous force and deep inertia,
you see how crumbled tons of stone, granulating further, inspire miles of evergreen

forest. What's more, from their summits we feed our delight in big pictures and see where we are, as far and as largely as possible.

What's more, any place-change alters our inner selves, a phenomenon as true of mental locales as terrestrial ones; hence, my maxim: context alters content—as, for example, when you happen to glance at a photo of the Andromeda galaxy. Well, when it comes to your inner content being altered by your context, the interface between words and our sense of this world is indeed a context—and the mind-place where writing happens. Figuratively speaking, it's an *ecotone,* the biologist's name for a transitional boundary between diverse communities of life-forms. Being transitional, it's also a zone where unexpectedly interesting things may happen, whether in life-forms or—again figuratively—within the life of language. In this latter sense, it becomes the site of what I whimsically call "my creationism."

As noted earlier, it's essentially a mode of self-organizing, which is to say self-evolving through writing. That's so, because the sort of ecotone created when language interacts with personal experience enables an *edge effect* begetting insights we can't reach any other way. In that ecotone, they somehow come to birth, often to our surprise. The very heart of a fine poetic image derives from precisely that inexplicable sort of surprise, which is why the true source of any poetic moment remains unknowable. Not all the life facts assembled by all of Emily Dickinson's biographers, for example, can ever begin to explain just why—among the innumerable possibilities—a particularly telling word or phrase just came to her. Nor, in all likelihood, could she.

Whether the writing be poetry or prose, that truth holds. Somehow, some way, in the word/life precinct I'm calling an ecotone, our inner content is altered—more subtly, to be sure, than when we swap mountains for seashore, or leave an office for the outdoors, or step from a city street into a barroom . . . but altered nonetheless— toward a special receptivity. That's why opening yourself to receive from your "self" what is accessible only within that ecotone can become a mode of self-creationism. You're not just leaning back in your chair and letting words happen; you're leaning forward, seeking whatever proves truest. And every seriously written result subtly alters who you are.

Obviously, the simple fact of spoiling the whiteness on a sheet of paper doesn't confer mystic powers. It does, however, enable the natural magic in language, which can and will happen for anyone who cares enough to take pains. A centuries-old saying about sloppy penmanship applies just as truly to the writing process: "Easy writing's curs't hard reading." And, if you've "a thing about words," caring enough to take pains isn't painful. In my kind of nonfiction, caring enough to take pains can involve travel, field work, notes, research, and much pondering. Even revision, which to non-writers must seem about as creative as sorting laundry, has real allure. Like a prospector sensing golden possibilities just round the next bend of a canyon, you're not driven but drawn.

Science and writing are two very different ways of knowing, yet writers and scientists are identical in being spurred further not by what they know but by what they don't know. Thus, they share a similar aim: discovery. But discovery of what? In my case, it's discovery of my relation to the natural world, which at the same time is self-discovery, inasmuch as the self is intimately bound to nature. The more we're aware of our kinship with the lowliest of life-forms, the higher our level of consciousness. Inasmuch as the human world is a parallel universe, I'd expect something similar to be true for writers of fiction, but on that topic I can't speak from personal experience.

Pains taken in following where your passion leads may seem out of all proportion to the modest result, so a skeptic could reasonably ask me, for example, "Why rack up lots of mileage, whether driving or hiking, just to write an essay?" Well, as the poet Wallace Stevens put it, in his poem, "Table Talk": "One likes what one happens to like." Still, for all that line's nonchalant tone, he knew well that a liking for discovery isn't a trivial urge.

That's because the most intriguing aspect to putting words on paper is, as I've said, their natural magic in causing insights to happen. As every writer knows, not only can they occur, but they invariably do. What's more, adventuring into the language/experience ecotone can produce passages better than you are, passages so good that the person you were—before so doing—couldn't have written them. In poetry, Robert Frost called that sort of result "a lucky hit," but, as golfer Jack Nicklaus put it, "I notice the more I practice the luckier I get."

Yet nothing is more common than letting our preconceptions falsify what we see; hence, the need for open eyes and an open mind. The layperson says, "Snow is white," whereas a landscape painter says, "Look more carefully, and you'll see color." The history of science can be written as a history of preconceptions overcome. In refusing to be informed by what's everywhere evident in the world of nature, the dogma-bound mind alters what's observed rather than being altered by it. To a surprising degree, what we see depends on who we are.

I once thought to tease a gung-ho motorcyclist by asking his reaction to *The Wild Ones* (1953), a film in which Marlon Brando plays the leader of a biker gang behaving like goons. "Oh," he said, oblivious to the hooligan aspect, "there were a few Harleys, but," in a disappointed tone, "they were mostly foreign makes. A lot of Kawasakis and Hondas, one or two Suzukis."

As is true of any art, serious writing is invariably moral, though the last person to understand "moral" in that context would likely be a Creationist. Art's opposition to any and all petrifaction of spirit is a moral opposition. Even one's style becomes a matter of conscience. Young writers may take awhile to learn what a vital role conscience plays in any craft, but "vital" is the right word. Sidney Bechet, a jazz great of the previous century, said as much in talking about his kind of music: "There cain't be no lyin.' It's got to come from the heart." In writing well, truth to what you actually see and feel, not what you think you *should* see and feel . . . well, that's crucial.

Your style can't be everyone's cup of tea, but it should at least be your own. Pee Wee Russell, a jazz clarinetist, explained his often deliberately raw playing with a frankness I quite like: "The note I blow may be the wrong note for anyone else, but it's the right note for me."

My moving to Colorado's mountains offers a case in point. I soon tried expressing in what I hoped might be poems some sense of our species' relation to that depth and breadth. Mountains didn't spur me to any hymns of praise, though my affair with them was, yes, love at first sight, but in an anti-Romantic way well apart from "magnificence" and "grandeur" and suchlike terms of the overcrowded sublime.

Roving alone amid the blind power of their granite upheavals felt precariously awesome in the root sense of the word. To be one brief creature surrounded by the thrust of such implicit force, as tremendous as it was pitilessness, epitomized our human situation. Though I reveled in my high-country rambles, I never for a moment sentimentalized what was so nakedly apparent there. So I wrote what expressed those powerfully mixed feelings.

Critics on the East Coast, however, tend to be dismissive of writing done by anyone in the intermountain West, regardless of tone or intent. I say they "tend" in that direction, but others have put it more bluntly. No less a poet and critic than Kenneth Rexroth—whose distinguished career has been honored at an award ceremony in our nation's capital—once remarked on that regional bias. "Easterners hold unshakably to their opinion that poetry set in the West amounts to mere bear shit on the trail."[4] As if the terrain between Chicago and San Francisco were not a place? Maybe it was beginner's luck that my first book of poetry found an East Coast publisher willing to bring out *Climbing into the Roots*. Luckily, its poems hadn't included any bear scat.

Every painter knows that drawing well and painting well depend on learning to see. Just looking, however, isn't seeing. Most people own two feet, though few ever study one in the way you must, if you're to draw a passably good foot. As John Constable, the English landscape painter observed, "We see nothing till we truly understand it." Thus, the better to see the human body, artists study anatomy. Like the visual arts, writing is a way of seeing and seeing into; thus—as I now say yet again—it's a way of discovering.

One day, while walking under a sky's high-country blue and the leaves of an aspen grove turned October gold near Gothic, Colorado, it dawned on me that I was looking but not seeing. What I looked at was mere scenery. That was so because, geologically and botanically, I understood less about what surrounded me than an earthworm does about the Big Dipper. I resolved to learn. That resolution soon extended to other regions of the West.

For example, bemused by my fascination with the ruins of the ancient Pueblo peoples (whom we call the Anasazi) of the Four Corners region in the Southwest—their excavated pots, scraps of woven cloth, yucca-fiber sandals, turquoise beads, and burial sites—I asked myself, "What's the attraction? Why do I drive hundreds of miles to pore over their long-since abandoned watch towers and dwellings?" I decided to write my way to the answer. Between reading and seeing, travel and long thought, I produced a short book, *Reaching Keet Seel: Ruin's Echo and the Anasazi*. Only after exploring in body and words those sites and artifacts left by the ancient ancestors of today's Pueblo people did I arrive at answers to that "Why?"

The attraction was kinship, yes, but with an affection I'd never have felt so deeply without the kind of "being there," which is writing.

That's partly because, despite this electronically mediated world, I happen—like many of us—still to live in a reciprocal landscape, though not nearly so intimately as did the Anasazi. In that land of little rain, to borrow Mary Austin's famous phrase, their relation to Sun and Moon, to creeks and seeps, to the Southwest's juniper and piñon pines, bighorn sheep, sandy soil and red stone was so life-and-death crucial it fused people and place. They became each other. Their Hopi and Zuñi and Acoma and easternmost descendants along the Rio Grande still agree. What they are is where they are, with the reverse proving equally true.

Slowly, my regard for places of the interior West fused with written words to become my way of being in the world. Their inter-animation is explained by the phrase cited earlier, "context alters content." For me, the life-path of its transactions hasn't led to a closed circle but, I hope, a rising spiral.

Oddly enough, it was while trying to cross Rome's Piazza Barberini at rush hour that I first learned with a jolt how greatly my years in a Western context had changed my inner content.

During my grad school days and before leaving Illinois, I had won a Fulbright to study in Italy, the country of time made human, layered deeper in history than any lasagna. With our infant Timothy, Anne and I lived for a while in a Perugian house whose medieval foundations had been laid on remnants of Perugia's Etruscan wall, itself laid with massive stone blocks many centuries before Christ—all of which suited my Big Picture nature. But I digress.

Back to Piazza Barberini and a trivial incident occurring after I'd lived twenty years at the foot of the Rockies.

Italians mistakenly think their national sport is soccer. It's traffic. Any rush hour in one of Rome's wide piazzas features Romans enacting Thomas Hobbes's view of pre-civilized humanity as "all against all." And how. In the evening around quitting time, the piazza before me was a manic vortex of cars, honking horns, and the noxious vapors from leaded gasoline. In the madding herd were daredevil Alfa Romeos, suicidal Vespas and motorbikes tearing the air to shreds, along with mousey little Fiats almost outroaring Rome's buses. One busload grazed me, as I looked up at its windows of winter faces—wan commuters scanning newspapers or numbly staring out the windows.

At long intervals, I had lived in little Fiesole, a tiny village above Florence, and Florence itself for extended stays, so had seen that city on the Arno go from relatively few cars to gridlock. Eight *intense* days of apartment hunting in Rome had, however, run my nerves ragged. It was rainy, I had a backache, and the apartments I'd been checking out weren't suited to my robust pair of teenage sons. I had hoped living in Rome would give them a taste of city life, so unlike Boulder and rock climbing.

Alas, it was I whom Piazza Barberini wised up. In its bumper-to-bumper piazza, with din and fumes an order of magnitude more daunting than in Firenze, I was not at full heroic strength.

Twice I set forth to cross, then startled back to the curb. Midway in my third attempt, between one step and the next, I came closer than ever in my life to freaking out, a blithering basket case right there as gaping pedestrians streamed past me. And had an awakening: "You can't take this any more, you're a Coloradan."

Ever since, it's grown all the truer. Out of the American West I'm a much dwindled thing, not really me. Even back in my native ploughlands, now mono-cropped by agribusiness yet still so abundantly green and fertile compared to our sunburnt lands west of the hundredth meridian, I'm completely irrelevant.

To a lesser extent, that contextual factor changed Anne, too. An Illinoisan like me, her reaction to mountains began as trepidation. As I said, we honeymooned in Colorado in 1958—on $175 and a Texaco credit card good for gas only. At our very first stop in the Rockies, Anne was leery of stepping from our new second-hand two-door Chevy "tu-tone." Wanting to snap a photo of the mountain view, I'd parked us at a pullover wide enough for an eighteen wheeler, but the height scared her anyway. Too spooked by the drop-off below, she wouldn't leave the car. "I'm afraid, if I do get out . . . I'll just float off over the edge."

Decades later, during a summer spent driving round Europe, we began laughing at ourselves every time we got near mountains. The more Coloradan they felt, the quicker our city-stressed spirits rose with the terrain. No sooner had our rental Peugeot begun climbing into the montane relief of forested ridgelines around, say, Chamonix or Gubbio or Montepulciano than Anne would contentedly exhale and say, "Ah-h-h! Now this is more like it." Me, too.

Context does indeed change content. Not only mountains and wide open spaces contextualize a person. The thought, discipline, and effort required to produce a good piece of writing does so as well and creates a slightly enhanced version of the author. I don't say it adds a whole cubit to her or his stature, but it does amount to an augmentation of self.

Or will, if we allow it to happen. Unfortunately, a belief system dependent on dogma and a closed world does not. Such systems favor lockstep and denial over openness and self-evolving.

Simply a blank sheet of paper can become the site of a potential context, which begins to alter slightly, even organize, your inner content. To analogize a bit, it can be catalyst, as was the baseball diamond in the Kevin Costner movie *Field of Dreams* (1989).

In that film, a young Iowa farmer (played by Costner) is haunted by a mysterious voice telling him, "If you build it, he will come." In defiance of all practicality and common sense, the farmer takes valuable acreage out of production and creates a fine baseball diamond out of his valuable cornfield. Soon its eerie allure leads to the ghostly emergence of legendary baseball players long-dead. Drawn to that diamond, they come alive again, bringing life to the field with their throwing, running, hitting, and banter. And, sure enough, among them is the very hitter the farmer had most wanted to see, Shoeless Joe Jackson, of the Chicago White Sox. Although the film is shamelessly sentimental, the erstwhile outfielder in me loved it. What's more, its central image can be seen as a parallel to that ecotone I've been talking about.

The hardest part of writing is overcoming the blank whiteness of the first page. Once begun, inertia gives way to interest verging on an allure distantly akin to what drew those apparitional athletes to Iowa. Onto the field of the page, hidden facets of your most considerate self appear and are drawn to a self-organizing kind of play. So am I saying, "If you just scribble, they will come?" No way. To claim that blank paper is a sure-fire field of dreams would be silly. However, if you care and take care, insightful—even surprising—relationships between the self and significant facets of your subject will begin showing up there, guaranteed. Especially if you like sentences.

NOT SO GREAT DEBATE

FOR MY ANNOUNCED showdown with Binford Pyle, I turned up on schedule ready for action, or so I thought. True, I had absolutely no debate experience and knew as little of the fundamentalist mind as it knows of Darwin and Wallace. So what? Biological fact was firmly on my side, wasn't it?

On entering a large vestibule, I found dozens of people studying Creationist displays and a wide screen overhead flashing a projected sequence of anti-Darwinian power points. Their techno-effect was unexpectedly hip. "Hm-m," I thought, "and me with only a few handwritten notes." The church's Baptist congregation, drawn from one of Denver's working-class suburbs, would surely be impressed by the electronic implication of cutting-edge info. Already I felt a bit daunted.

As each slide brightened, then dissolved into the next one, I hadn't time to read more than a few. Yet, visually snappy as they were, they paraded the same old junk-science and untruths which, nonetheless, have found a home in the hearts of countless devotees who take the biblical description of creation literally.

Why do we believe the unbelievable? Agreed, the answer is obvious: because we want to, but saying so addresses only the why, not the how. It's the how which intrigues me.

No sooner had I left the vestibule's displays and entered the church proper, where adult murmuring mingled with adolescent chatter, than I became dismayed by the sight of so many young faces, including many children. I'd assumed the entire audience would be grown-ups. To undercut parental authority was the last thing I, with my straight-arrow Midwestern upbringing, wanted to do. That reluctance led me to scrap the main argument of my opening remarks: a critique of the fundamentalist dogma on the *Bible*'s inerrancy, plus remarks on the ungodly blood lust of the God its Old Testament describes. Intellectually, my spur of the moment decision to back off was indefensible. I didn't care. Children's respect for their parents' judgment seemed more important, so I chose to extemporize.

On a brightly lit, carpeted platform, Binford Pyle and I sat opposite, each of us behind a small table covered with red cloth. Though Pyle was a man of large girth, he carried his weight well, was soberly attired in a dark blue suit, and made quite a good appearance, while the open laptop before him continued the cutting-edge implications. These he further enhanced by setting it on the podium each time his turn came to speak or rebut. My few handwritten notes seemed so slight by comparison I ditched them.

From the Internet I had learned of Pyle's speaking engagements and videos; and learned, too, of his conceiving and leading, with others, something called Scriptural Tours in science museums, so as to correct the un-biblical information infesting such places. Learned as well of his connection to the Farview Academy, which trains young fundamentalists.

Between us at the podium in marked contrast to Mr. Pyle stood our moderator, a man in his late twenties, one Jeremy Higgins. What with his abundant beard, flowing brown hair, and bulky figure, the teddy-bear aspect made his role as the church's Youth Director seem natural. Into the microphone he explained how the debate would proceed. Each of us would give a ten-minute opening argument. These would be followed by rebuttals, the first of eight minutes, then one of five minutes. We'd each make five-minute closing arguments, after which we'd take questions from the audience.

Just before Pyle and I mounted the platform we stood momentarily face-to-face long enough for me to ask if he took the creation story in the Book of Genesis literally. His reply was edgy, as if long since weary of that question. "The Creator" he said, "made the world in six days of twenty-four hours."

Temptation overcame me. I asked, "What took him so long?"

He didn't answer that one, so, after an ominous pause, I tried again. "Well . . . how can you tell whether a given biblical passage is figurative or literal?"

In the same dismissive tone, he said, "You can tell by the context," which, on the one hand, is true enough but, on the other, sounds like dealer's choice. I was about to press the point when the moderator asked us to take our places.

To avoid being typecast as one of those university professors fond of destroying young souls with their godless ideas, I wore my cowboy-style vest woven with Indian designs. Furthermore, I topped it off with a black, broad-brimmed Stetson and choke strap, such as bad guys always wore in the dime movies of my boyhood Saturday afternoons back in Illinois.

During Mr. Higgins's preliminaries, I doffed the Stetson, then, when my turn came to speak, put it back on and, in a bantering manner, began with something like the following: "Lest anybody be confused, my hat should clarify the situation. Creationists here can relax. Though Mr. Pyle isn't wearing a white hat, we know the man in the black hat always loses. To simplify things further, I advise those who are satisfied with their beliefs not to credit a word I say." Then, after pointing out the impossibility of a debate between faith and fact, sketched my position without raising my voice. Especially with an audience of working-class Baptists, soft-spoken was the only way to go.

Besides, Creationists can never lose, owing to the well-known fact that Scripture cannot err, which is proven by its being divinely inspired, which is, in turn, proven by the fact that people who lived eons ago have said so. Even as God's words have undergone numerous translations and editions as the *Bible* moved forward as a book with many authors for many people, purposes, and cultures.

With that as bedrock, everything Creationism—including its clone, Intelligent

Design—has to say passes between twin pillars. The falsehood inscribed on one pillar reads thus: "Without the *Bible* and Christ, there can be no morality." The whopper chiseled into the other pillar says: "Evolution is atheistic." Binford Pyle bludgeoned us with those twin fallacies and implied the atheistic bent of evolution by saying, "Evolution claims nature is all there is." It, of course, does no such thing. Like all science it merely restricts itself to observable phenomena and testable evidence. Oddly, large numbers of lay persons interpret those limits as proof that science has it in for religion.

Saying that morality's impossible without the *Bible* and Christ requires not only perfect ignorance of the ancient world, but Creationism's foundational denial of our species' prehistory. Owing to the survival value of cooperative behavior within primate species, morality simply evolved—like everything else. Even our deities are better behaved now than they used to be.

"Evolved?" boggled Pyle, who insisted that the moral truth of the *Bible* is "eternal and unchanging." Such a remark made me wonder, "Has he read it?" Without such a moral absolute, he continued, "There would be no reason why I shouldn't wrap an airplane around myself and fly into a building."

Directing a baleful glare at the audience, he said angrily, "If you're an evolutionist and you're upset about 9/11, get over it." Considering our presumably decent congregation of believers, I forbore quoting on that topic of malevolence the comment by Steven Weinberg, a Nobel laureate in physics: "With or without religion, good people can behave well and bad people can do evil; but for good people to do evil— that takes religion."[1]

Though persons of goodwill can and often do strenuously disagree on an issue, Pyle's righteous indignation on all topics Darwinian seemed to be tinged with some darker animus. I wondered what his life had been before its born-again phase.

"All men," he said, "are flawed and must be restrained." The worse we are, the better for Pyle's exhorting our fallen natures to rise up from the muck. What good is a cure if there's no disease? Unsurprisingly, therefore, he insisted no mire could be blacker than that in the Darwinian morass. Later, however, he surprised me by backing off long enough to say, "Evolution doesn't *make* people wicked; people *are* wicked."

Would we humans, unless compelled by a divine Sky Cop to behave ourselves, lapse into bestiality? Oh, yes! In fact, this alleged degeneracy of humankind's post-lapsarian state seemed oddly dear to the man's heart and not just because he was selling the cure.

It's true the Pauline Epistles are pervaded by insistent references to our sinful flesh and Satan's activism among us. After all, Christianity's main claim is that our fallen species desperately needed a Redeemer. But Paul's better angel also moved him frequently to exhort his hearers on the value of their communal bond—and love. Could Pyle's gloomy view of our nature, I continued to wonder, have been rooted in himself as well as the *Bible?* At times in our debate—as if his hearers' salvation were imperiled—his body went rigid, and his nostrils flared while, like an accuser from the Holy Office of the Inquisition, his wrath-of-God eyes glowered warningly at the audience.

Whether he did so from personal truculence or religious zeal I couldn't know but had no doubt what my fate would be if he or any cult of like-minded zealots had the power to inflict rack and stake on misbelievers. I easily imagined them torching Joan of Arc to improve her character.

As Blaise Pascal knew well, what with his Europe's bloody wars of religion, "Men never do evil so fully and so happily as when they do it for conscience's sake."[2] Or, for that matter, so fully and happily as when they spread untruths.

Thanks to Binford Pyle, I now know that "racism is promoted by evolution," that morality comes from a Creationist worldview, whereas "evolution is inherently self-ish; it is self-centered and thrives on death." I also learned that "genocide becomes a natural outflowing of the evolutionary model when applied to human relations." Oh, all manner of Darwinian-induced degeneracy fueled his rancor. He spoke of evolution as if it weren't a science at all but a conspiracy so dangerous that some Creationists call it "devilution," a satanic cult roaming the world on cloven hooves and seeking the destruction of souls.

Most vividly of all, I remember his claim that an "evolutionist" is bound to con-
done Hitler's grisly eugenic experiments. That's as illogical as saying Pasteur would
favor germ warfare. I also recall how my eyes widened and mouth gaped when he
read a quote from Adolf Hitler by way of implying that the author of *Mein Kampf*
(1925) spoke for Darwinians! What's more, he twice followed former Texas Congressman Tom DeLay's lead in linking the bloody murders at Columbine High
School in Littleton, Colorado, in 1999, to the teaching of evolution: "Evolution kills
people," declared Binford Pyle. "If you don't believe me, just look at Columbine!"
Then he added, "Those two students learned their lessons well . . . and applied those
lessons appropriately."[3]

Given the time constraints on rebuttals, I couldn't begin to point out more than
a few absurdities in Mr. Pyle's stream of grievances. Certainly, the most dramatic
among them was his charge that Hitler's evolutionist worldview led to the Holocaust.

You may well ask, as I did, "How, pray tell, did it do that?"

It seems Darwin's "survival of the fittest" was the culprit. It had authorized *blitz-
krieg* and mass murder.[4] Such an inexhaustibly fallacious statement betrayed gross
ignorance of evolutionary fitness, *the* key concept in *On the Origin of Species* (1859).
Darwin did not say, as Binford Pyle explicitly claimed, that survival depends on
strength and cunning; rather, evolutionary fitness stems from an organism's ability
to adapt biologically to changing environmental conditions. Mighty dinosaurs may
perish and tiny mammals thrive.

The charge that Hitlerian evil was merely Darwinism in action has become
a favorite whopper among the Religious Right. In late August 2006, the Rev. D.
James Kennedy—dubbed by blogger Pam Spaulding "the Talibangelist titan of
Florida-based Coral Ridge Ministries"—offered TV viewers a sixty-minute documentary titled *Darwin's Deadly Legacy*. It hyped the false analogy between Nazi eugenics and Darwin's theory of natural selection, thus sharing Pyle's stunning mis-
conception of the theory he so decried.[5] Furthermore, selective breeding was an
ancient practice, so Nazi eugenics didn't need Darwin to inspire it. In point of fact,
World War II revealed the Nazi unfitness to survive, inasmuch as Nazism reduced

Germany to bombed-out ruins. Nazi unfitness, however, wasn't the kind Darwin was talking about.

As if to produce a crescendo effect, Mr. Pyle began totting up the separate body counts attributable to Hitler, Stalin, and Chairman Mao, with a bonus estimate of lives unborn, owing to Margaret Sanger's promotion of birth control. "That's over 190 million people," he said, "who have been purposely sacrificed on the altar of evolution!"

I flashed on a headline—DARWIN KILLS 190 MILLION—and reeled. But that wasn't the nadir. Either Pyle's misunderstanding or willful misrepresentation of the evolution he so deplored gave birth to this *pièce de résistance:* "If your brain evolves," he asked the audience, "how can you trust your own thinking?"

"At least," I thought but didn't say, "it would be headed in the right direction."

Our debate had become a carnival attraction. I was still tottering over evolution's Slaughter of the Innocents when Mr. Pyle informed the audience that, so long as I embraced evolution, I was destined for eternal torment. He said it grieved him that I was bound for hell, though I didn't hear grief in his tone.

Just then, and mercifully, the robust Mr. Higgins, our moderator and time-keeper, signaled an end to the fray and the beginning of a brief Q&A period. Without exception, the queries addressed specifically to me raised points I had already dwelt on in some detail. It was as if their memories had suppressed facts which these questioners did not want to know.

A sampling, given here in my paraphrase, indicates their drift. "How can an evolutionist be moral?" "How can intricate life-forms come from chaos without God's help?" "Is evolution a religion?" "Why can't a person believe in God *and* natural selection?" "Should evolution and creationism both be taught in schools?" "What about those fossils?" "Where did the universe come from?" "If you don't believe in anything, what happens when you die?"

In the milling about before leaving, most audience members—either from fatigue, shyness, or aversion—gave me a wide berth. Still, a heartwarming half-dozen came up to say—more in manner than words—that, for a Darwinian, I didn't seem such a bad sort. One shy young man had liked my low-key delivery. To another, my speaking offhandedly without notes or laptop had seemed something of a feat. An earnest young woman surprised me by expressing her surprise: that to illustrate various points I could quote scripture. Had she supposed evolutionists recoil from the *Bible* like vampires from a cross?

If nothing else, our not-so-great debate had at least brought me face to face with what I've called humanity's peculiar gift for believing the unbelievable. Besides, hadn't I predicted the man in the black hat always loses?

DEITIES ON THE CEILING AND THE THEOLOGY OF UP

FARCICAL AS IT WAS, that debate with Binford Pyle taught me more than I expected; mainly, the degree to which decades of university life had led me to take rational discourse for granted. Instead, what counted was one fact and one opinion.

The one fact was Pyle's ignorance of evolutionary science. In Pyle's case, it lent fervor to his inanities as if he truly believed them, which he apparently did. It also reminded me how effective bearing false witness can be when repeated again and again. And the one opinion? It was Pyle's axiomatic certainty that Holy Writ cannot err. As Oscar Wilde once said of the *Bible*, "When I think of all the harm that book has done, I despair of ever writing anything to equal it."

Yes, the *Bible* and *Qu'rân* are revered literary accounts, but they were produced—as noted earlier—by humans with less knowledge of our planet and universe than today's average fourth-grader. Projecting supernatural qualities onto sacred writings derives from our prehistoric past, whether the object be a rare pelt, hallowed tree, river, lake, sea, stone, scroll, or terrain. As for the latter, certain mountains have become sacred by means of our projections onto them, an instinctual response which accounts for what I call "the theology of up."

Up is where the gods and goddesses live. Always have and always will. Sky high. A hard-shell Creationist would cite biblical passages as the authority for our reverent upward glances, and doubtless that's a factor, but our evolutionary past goes stone ages deeper than scriptural acculturation. Mountains make us cock our heads back. The moment we do, an encoding millions of years old kicks in. Doesn't every tourist among towering sequoias or redwoods look way up and feel spiritual stirrings?

The reflex is automatic. What's more, we like it. Looking up involves us in a slight contextual change altering our inner content. A starry night, same difference. Yet such a change can occur simply as stepping from street noises into a church. Decades after I'd shelved the *Baltimore Catechism* and its God hypothesis, that fact was dramatically enacted in me during an aimlessly pleasant morning in France.

Within forty-eight hours of debarking from a British hydroplane at Calais, Anne and I found ourselves heading our rental Peugeot toward Amiens for no particular reason. During previous trips, we'd done our share of culture-vulturing. In France alone, you can self-improve till you drop. For this trip, however, our summer plan was to have no plan, just spur-of-the-moment whim. Despite my systematic cathedral-bagging in Italy, I somehow had never stepped inside a really impressive example of French Gothic. The sole exception had been the cathedral of Notre Dame on the Isle de France in Paris; venerable, yes, but disappointingly small, dark, and dingy.

Barely over the threshold of Amiens's great Gothic edifice (a cathedral about which I'd read nothing, thus expected nothing) my gaze was swept upward by the astonishing verticality of pillars along its nave. My suddenly in-taken breath made me so instantly medieval I let slip a long "Oh-h-h" with an awe that turned heads.

Looking up. That's how most churches work.

So do mountains. Deities have always taken to the high ground. Gods dwelling on heights is as old as the hills, with their two hyper-ancient reasons being Up and Big. Long before the ascent of our avatars from down on all fours to our two-footed way of getting around, Big and Up were, for survival purposes, pretty much the same thing. Bigger than me is usually taller as well and taller usually bigger. Big can hurt us, kill us. Better act humble with Big. Our earliest, lowliest, still-slithering forebears learned that the hard way and passed it on when they morphed into the fur-bearing line. Big and Up imply each other.

Isn't it hard not to take thunder personally? Lightning, too. After a near flash-and-crash, there's an inevitable millisecond of feeling some Mr. Big's on your case. Add height to size and you see why the worldwide affinity between deities and mountains came so naturally. Sacred mountains abound throughout the globe, four in the desert Southwest alone. There, villages of Hopi dancers still chant their welcome to katsina (or kachina) spirits, who seasonally descend from their home on the nearby San Francisco Mountains to visit the various Hopi pueblos. When it's time for the katsinas to return, these same performers re-assemble to dance and sing their gratitude.

As to big and tall, who has more visibly immanent power than a mountain? The rest is history, the evolutionary history of gods, arising from the fact that, among mammals—including talking ones—size usually affects dominance. Thanks to the U.S. Army having treated me to arctic indoctrination in Alaska, I chanced to see a sort of theological extension of that bigness factor enacted among fish-whapping grizzlies during a salmon run. A mid-size sow had just carried her catch of a fat salmon off to one side of the roaring whitewater when, lo! along came a bigger male whose looming presence said, "I think I'd like that one myself."

What to do? The inevitable. What we all do if we know what's good for us. He being bigger, she let him have her catch. Better to lose a fish than risk worse. At the time, I was a callow twenty-two, knew little about the ancient world, and thus didn't see that bear transaction as enacting the origin of human sacrificing to the gods. When Greeks poured forth a few ounces of wine onto the soil as a libation to, say, Apollo, or wrapped choice cuts of ram in fat and burnt them as an offering to Zeus, they were—in a ritual way—doing the same as that grizzly sow: giving some so as not to lose more or all. Just as every god is born of our fears and wishes, each ritual gift or prayer to a deity says the same, "Please help—but, if you won't help, please don't hinder."

For Hebrews the same fusion was true. Sacrificing to Yahweh or Eloim aimed both to placate and solicit. In childhood, I was taught to "offer up" all manner of trivial "sacrifices," whether pleasures forgone or pain endured. Doing so would either lessen God's wrath at my sinful nature or earn me some bonus points, maybe both. The taproot of what passes for "worship" is precisely that: giving to get. Up there in Alaska, though, all that sow seemed to get for her salmon was breathing room.

Implausible as it may seem, for precisely those up-and-down reasons astronomical science developed long before geology. What was underfoot was beneath our notice.[1] In 1637, René Descartes (1596–1650), often called the father of modern philosophy, remarked on the superiority of up in an essay on meteors: "We are naturally more inclined to admire things above us than those on our level or below. . . ."[2]

A figurative use of "level" makes it equally true in discussing the origin of deities. My explanation of that origin is bound to be dismissed as beneath the dignity of anything so lofty as a god. "Surely," a reader must feel, "true explanation of something so tremendous can't be that simple." Such a thought makes the time-honored but erroneous assumption that great effects must have great causes. Further on, in the chapter titled "The Geo-Theology of Down," I discuss and cite the disproof of that assumption by the eighteenth-century earth scientist James Hutton (1726–1797), the first to understand that enormous geological effects have "little causes, long continued."

When new to teaching, I naively supposed universities—those citadels of intellect— were wholly exempt from our brutish past till I began noticing that, at my own university, the people running things (back then almost entirely male) tended to be taller than the average faculty member. I say they *tended* to be so. If feminism eventually changes the setup, it'll be to authority held by taller-than-average women.

Isn't it still true that the average female mates with a man she can look up to rather than down on, as if a yardstick could measure personal stature! In reaching the most serious social decision we'll ever make, doesn't choosing a mate partly on the basis of height boggle the mind? Me, I tower above my wife, Anne, by a good two inches.

Furthermore, up/down associations pervade our figurative references to values stated as degrees of height or its lack. Ultimately, that has its origin in the spine of *Homo erectus*, whose vertebral column became the original axis of moral values. Surely, as every newborn human finally grows strong enough to lift its head, literal and figurative rectitude followed our turning bipedal.

This surmise would seem far-fetched indeed, if not for the anthropological fact that bipedalism is widely held to have been a crucial juncture in the evolutionary "rise" of *Homo sapiens*. Simple as up and down, the spine's verticality gave rise, in turn, to our moral spectrum with its descending gradations from superior to inferior.

Heaven is, therefore, highest, hell lowest. In olden times, altars were higher than ground level and are so to this day. Clergy preach from the height of a pulpit, and the climactic gesture of a Catholic Mass is the elevation of the host. In Medieval Europe, the original space-race featured rivalry between cities in building the highest steeple or bell tower. Especially in that Age of Faith, a like rivalry led to saint-races, as competing towns urged Catholic Rome to elevate this or that pious citizen to the rank of saint. Once canonized, the saint became both a point of local pride and a talisman.

As if echoing the gradations between celestial and infernal opposition, we hold upright behavior to be admirable, low behavior deplorable. The one straight, the other, if not crooked, at least inclined away from the good. We speak of lower and higher animals, of low people and high-minded ones. In choosing between alternatives, we consider the upside and downside of each. The lowest behavior may be beneath contempt, the highest praised to the skies. A pop singer be "super" or abysmal, just as any politician may rise or sink in the polls.

Nowhere is the verticality of values more significant than in the Book of Genesis and the story of the Fall, which caused Eve and Adam to be evicted from the Garden of Eden. An almighty downer indeed.

Months before my debate with Binford Pyle, I had bought one of his videos, *Science Flim Flams of Credulous People* (1996). Its title revealed his penchant for turning the tables on gainsayers who accuse Creationism of suppressing crucial realities. In content and style, the video's footage offered artlessly preachy stuff, with its best scene coming in a trailer showing Binford Pyle as leader of a Scriptural Tour at a city zoo. He asked his youthful group, "Why is the tiger fenced off from the other animals?" And his answer? It was one I had been keen to hear. "Sin," said Binford Pyle.

Okay, I thought, so the answer is sin and recalled his relish in the fact of our innate depravity. But how, we may wonder, in the Garden of Eden before the Fall, had its tigers survived a meatless diet of plants with carnivore teeth? Well, hard-core Creationists know that present-day carnivores were, before the Fall, vegetarians. In Genesis 1:30, the Creator says, "And to every beast of the earth, and to every fowl of the air, and to everything that creepeth upon the earth, wherein there is life, I have given every green herb for meat; and it was so."[3] Obviously, Pyle wouldn't say that sin caused today's tiger fangs to *evolve* from the pre-Lapsarian grinder-teeth of vegetarian ruminants and other browsers. Prior to our debate, I had meant to question him on that point, then in the heat of things forgot all about it. But I digress.

Virtue's vertical axis is further reinforced by degrees of light and darkness given a moral value. Heaven's altitude makes it necessarily brightest, while hell's infernal murk broods at the opposite pole, with actions below the midpoint tending to be shady.

After all, didn't our birth deliver into the light a little phototropic mammal? I always thought "reaching for the moon" a mere cliché till one evening I actually saw my sister's latest infant trying again and again to grasp the full moon visible from its crib. One baby often reaches for another baby's brightest part, the eyes, since our hard-wired reflex toward brightness works as innately as our response to up. In speaking of intelligence, we use degrees of light to quantify it, with a verticality of implicitly upward gradations from dim through blank to bright, to brilliant, to dazzling. Among Greeks, Apollo was many things, but as the immortal most often associated with intellect he was also a sun god, brightness and altitude fused.

Throughout Europe we find deities colorfully painted on the ceiling. Where else but up? In Renaissance palaces, it's true, they're frequently pagan gods and goddesses of the Greco-Roman tradition, with the palace's ducal owner often shown among them. Depicted deifically, his painted person floats overhead, enhanced by wafting robes and luminous cloud effects, while winged cherubs hover about him and his celestial tendency.

I've admired many such upward apotheoses, some in fresco, some in the colored-glass tesserae of mosaics, but nowhere have art and up fused so impressively as on the world's most famously deific ceiling, that of the Sistine Chapel in Rome. Once, by contrivance, I admired it quite alone for a full ten minutes before the murmuring herds of tour guides and their clients arrived like a cattle drive to make full concentration impossible. The spectacle of hundreds craning their necks to look straight up made Michelangelo—who, even while he lived, was called *il divino*—easily the most impressive creator on the ceiling.

WILLIAM PALEY'S VERY WONDERFUL WATCH

THE DEAD SEA SCROLLS have reached us in tatters. Apollo's rubbled temple at Delphi survives mainly as memory. The marble arms of the goddess Venus as sculpt by Milo can't reach us at all, long lost, like the original noses of nearly every ancient statue. Yet the Reverend William Paley's (1743–1805) watch has come down to us unimpaired. Has any artifact ever survived *such* a series of users as that fabulous timepiece? Furthermore, it not only keeps time devoutly as ever it did but shows nary a scratch nor least sign of wear, not even thumb-burnish.

Yet the thing was already well over 2,000 years old when our perambulating cleric—in his 1802 best-seller—wrote of coming upon it while strolling the Lincolnshire heath. In fact, he describes his conjectural find at the very outset of that popular volume, *Natural Theology, or Evidences of the Existence and Attributes of the Deity Collected from the Appearances of Nature*. If in crossing the heath—as he tells us in the book's beginning—he should be asked how one or another of its stones came to be underfoot, "I might possibly answer, that, for anything I knew to the contrary, it had lain there for ever; nor would it perhaps be very easy to show the absurdity of this answer." So much for a stone.

"But," he continues, "suppose I had found a *watch* upon the ground." Reason would have told him that, unlike the stone, it had been contrived for some end. That, in turn, meant "the watch must have had a maker," and its cogs and springs were the work of "an artificer or artificers, who formed it for the purpose which we find it actually to answer, who comprehended its construction and designed its use." Throughout his *Natural Theology*, Paley applies the inference of a maker to everything and to human anatomy, in particular, even extending that same shaky logic to the physiology of plants.

Inevitably, his crowning instance was the human eye, thereby furnishing Creationists with an anti-Darwinian ace of spades trumping all other cards in the deck, the one argument they never tire of expounding. In fact, it is their one and only argument: "Someone must have done this."[1] As noted in a previous chapter, it's always some *one*, never some *thing*. Thus, the immaterial watch has been handed down from Creationist to Creationist and thence to proponents of so-called Intelligent Design (ID), in whose keeping it's still going strong.

Not only that. As it did in the devout hands of the loveable and nature-loving Reverend Paley, this marvelous watch aids Creationists by foisting onto nature a Divine Horologer whose hand their junk-science pretends to discover. Which is but human. Before the rise of science, most persons and tribes explained unusual events in terms of spirits or deities. A thinker Paley indeed was, as well as a gifted writer. Inevitably, therefore, his *Natural Theology* insisted on seeing everywhere among stones, plants, and animals "the necessity . . . of an intelligent designing mind for . . . the forms which organized bodies bear." As if his pious reading of Genesis had nothing to do with what he saw.

Plainly, despite the chest-thumping by ID's leaders about "Darwinism in crisis," Creationism gone digital merely swaps the watch for some intricate molecules. With a sprinkling of hocus-pocus mathematics whose fallacious methods have been exposed by persons versed in probability theory, they "prove" that such molecules could not be the result of chance.[2] But this digitalized *déjà vu* is no more the brain child of ID than it was of Paley.

A generation before that worthy was born, Paley's indestructible timepiece had passed into the hands of a Dutch writer, Bernard Nieuwentyt (1654–1718), whose book of 1716 put it to the same pious uses. Nor was Nieuwentyt by any means its first finder. The Roman writer Cicero drew a similar analogy between a wondrous armillary sphere constructed by one Posidonius, Cicero's teacher at Rhodes, who devised a mechanism which modeled the movement of the sun and moon and the planets. "If this were brought even to primitive Britain," wrote Cicero, "no one there would doubt it was the product of reason. Surely the original thus modeled proclaims even more loudly that it is the product of a divine mind."[3] The Reverend Paley couldn't have said it better.

Cicero then followed this clincher with another golden oldie still favored by Creationists: "Anyone who believes that the world is the result of chance," writes the Roman, "might as well believe that if you threw enough letters of the alphabet into an urn and shook them out onto the ground you would produce a copy of the Annals of Ennius."[4] Clearly, this is the distant ancestor of Creationism's monkey at a typewriter. What are the primate's chances of producing the text of *Hamlet* by poking away at the keyboard? Well, they say, the odds against a world with no Creator are improbably higher. Ditto for the odds against chance begetting a fancy molecule, much less the wonders within a single living cell.

What anti-Darwinians refuse to understand is that evolution isn't driven by sheer chance. Its processes of self-organization depend on a continuous interaction between chance and natural law. In other words, each successful modification of a life-form results from the interplay between randomness and functionality.

Though Charles Darwin admired Paley's mind and style, Darwin's theory of natural selection should have long ago finished off this false if time-honored analogy between watch and eye, or between watch and molecule, watch and bacterial flagellum, or watch and blood chemistry. I say "false analogy," because, as the poet e. e. cummings has reminded us, "a world of made is not a world of born." A fact too obvious for words, except that Creationists keep failing to notice the difference.

And not only they. Paley's analogy between watch and microbe, or watch and hummingbird, or watch and the entire universe, illogical as it is, continues in perennial favor with the greater part of humankind and probably always will. So much for "common sense."

An equally ancient corollary of the understandable but wishful assertion that there can't be highly intricate design in nature without an Intelligent Designer is the axiomatic and far more ancient assumption that nature's creations must perforce come to birth through a top-down process. About 2,600 years ago, the Greek thinker Xenophanes put it this way: "The greater cannot be brought into being by the lesser."[5] You can almost see Creationists nodding their heads in assent, murmuring, "Indeed, it must be so. Only the higher can beget the lower." As a Creationist youngster, I once nodded and murmured, right along with them. "Heck yes. Anybody can see that."

A century or two after Xenophanes, the Greek philosopher Zeno of Elea (ca. 490–450 B.C.), living in what is now southern Italy, affirmed a similar self-evident truth: "Nothing inanimate can generate something that is animate."[6] Here, too, Creationists could not agree more. Zeno, however, immediately went on to affirm another axiom they would find less to their liking: "But the world generates things that are animate; therefore the world is animate."[7]

Whoa! Time out! An animate world? That's downright pantheism, which, to the Creationist is damnable. And against common sense.

Common sense certainly plays a role in science. Nonetheless, what I didn't know as a child Creationist is that the early histories of astronomy, biology, chemistry, and physics embraced many similarly self-evident verities turning out to be fictions. In science, when it comes to common-sense axioms, you got to know "when to hold 'em and when to fold 'em."

THE DARWINIAN DIVINITY CALLED TIME

INEVITABLY, REACTION TO the natural world is very different from a response to art, though appreciation of any fine thing, whether a barn swallow or a drawing by Matisse, leaves me impressed by their maker.

When it comes to mega-galaxies, osprey, or, for example, the complex culture of leaf-cutting ants, that maker is time: the vast, inscrutable reach of it. My stunned wonder at the echolocation of bats can trigger a sort of free-fall astonishment, the mind plummeting back through the evolutionary epochs needed to develop an ultrasound system so exquisitely and finely tuned.

Lying all about and within us, nature's smallest details abound with time's creativities. Every strawberry for my breakfast granola has bedecked itself with minuscule time capsules disguised as seeds. That's cunning indeed, but time's genius as encapsulated by each human cell staggers the mind. Our cells are more impressive than we are. Yet they'd be nothing without water, that most versatile of all elements.

Few sights give rise to such a fusion of joy and awe as the wild, waterfall descent of torrents leaping off cliffs, and no water runs clearer or more pristine than that which I often draw from a high-country stream in the Rockies. Nor, when gulped from my brimming steel cup, does any water taste so much like drinking the sky. Yet, fresh as it seems, all water—whether dammed, developed, polluted, or just divert-ed—is both young as the morning dew and more ancient than the nameless moun-tains it epochs ago melted to nothing. Older than the planet itself, water shares in all our secrets while keeping its own. Nothing's so common; yet, among the many elements in our bodies, water's simple mystery remains the least fathomable.

Seen that way, imagination can wander billions of years within a droplet. Or, in pondering raven plumage—with its barbules, barbicels, and hooklets so cunning-ly contrived from an original squiggle of keratin—can be rapt by the depth of time in a feather.

Our human brain is—so far as we know—the most complex object in the uni-verse, but its range is too helplessly shallow for sounding such deeps. Might as well stand on a hilltop and try to see around the world or try charting ridges and valleys on the floor of the Pacific Ocean with a twenty-foot rope.

There's also the fact that, very probably, our sensory equipment may be severely limited to what's actually present all around us. Our species might well have evolved eyes otherwise excellent but unable to detect color. With everyone knowing only a monochrome world, color would have remained forever inconceivable. Yet it would have been all around us. Doubtless there's more to our world than we have sensory apparatus enough to perceive. What we look on may be meager indeed, compared to what's there. If our species endures long enough, then creating Time, as Shakespeare surmised, may evolve sensory gifts presently unimaginable.

Unfortunately, the extent of gone time, because it is literally unimaginable, remains unreal for all too many, especially the anti-Darwinians. Since 1982, Gal-lup has polled U.S. citizens on the origin of *Homo sapiens:* "Which of the following statements comes closest to your views on the origin and development of human be-ings—human beings have developed over millions of years from less advanced forms of life, but God guided this process; human beings have developed over millions of years from less advanced forms of life, but God had no part in this process; [or] God created human beings in pretty much their present form at one time in the last 10,000 years or so?"

From 1982 through 2008, an average of forty-five percent of respondents chose the latter, all-God opinion, with 37.4 percent believing God guided evolution and 11.7 percent saying God had no role in the evolutionary process.[1]

But "at one time *in the last 10,000 years* or so?" Thus, God created us no longer ago than, say, the end of the last Ice Age? Already by then even the remote landforms of North America had begun to be populated! (And almost certainly much earlier.) Surely, it's the immeasurable spans of evolutionary time such believers cannot conceive of. Nor can they conceive how, to cite a seminal phrase by the eighteenth-century gentleman geologist James Hutton—"Little causes, long continued"—could have wrought in all life-forms and landforms such enormous effects.

"Long continued" in the case of Earth's *life* comes to some 3.5 billion years.[2] Those who don't believe the human eye could have evolved are incredulous partly because they have no clear concept of the words "million" and "billion." Suppose your doctor should look up from her clipboard to say, "I'm afraid the tests are not good." Naturally you'll wonder, "How long have I got?"

Answering your thought, she breaks the news, "You have, I'm sorry to say, only a million seconds to live." Time enough to drive to your favorite coffee house for a last latte? Yes and to spare. Almost twelve full days.

Now imagine, having misread her own writing, she corrects herself. "Did I say 'million'? Sorry 'bout that! I meant to say billion. Give or take a few, you've got a billion seconds before the end."

How many more days would that give you? Plenty. In fact, thirty-two years. Despite all the bandying of large numbers in the media, people can't grasp how "long continued" a span of 3.5 billion years really is. Yet three minutes with a calculator easily proves what I've said.

Apropos of our natural world as imagined by the average Joe or Josephine, a Harris poll reported that only fifty percent of those questioned know that Earth goes around the sun and takes a year to do it.[3] Only half! The other day, while chatting with Brad McLain, a young scientist doing outreach educational programs with the NASA-backed Space Science Institute, I protested, "Surely, that percentage cannot possibly be true, can it?"

"Oh, my," he said, pitying my naiveté, "you have no idea. We deal with that and worse on a regular basis."

In later questioning a public school teacher who was pursuing her M.A. in education, my smile congealed on finding she didn't know our solar system is much, much closer to Earth than even the very nearest star. Reading my eyes, she huffed dismissively, "Well, I don't pretend to know science."

"That's not science," I said. "It's where you are."

As I've confessed, of all the elements I find time and water the most magical. Thanks to Hutton's "little causes, long continued," they and a fistful of minerals are what I'm made of. Out here in the erosional American West, where time and land wear the same face, water's visible absence has shaped rugged summits, crags, cliffs, alluvial fans. The Southwest's buttes, hardpan, arroyos, and canyons are so many variations on time petrified. I live in a mountain region flattened epochs ago by wind and weather to a land of low relief whose summits rose no higher than dunes. As they have in the past, the present-day Rockies will come down again. It's part of our where.

As it happens, just this past February my town was dusted over by Arizona sand fine as time, blown here from many hundreds of miles away. Its siliceous substance, micro-finely divided, felt between finger and thumb more like flour than grit and lent a faint tan to our snow. All across Boulder thousands of parked cars wore that tan coating of the geological time, which will eventually level our mountains.

Elsewhere I've written about a line between strata deep in the Grand Canyon from which 1.2 billion years of stone once there were eroded clean away! Having earlier given the word "billion" some content, let's now consider this: the nucleus in each of our cells encloses staggering numbers of nucleotides paired within every

DNA molecule. If you enjoy a thought to get lost in, how much time do you suppose went into contriving such a savvy, all-purpose assemblage?

Then there's cosmic time, which Darwin and Wallace could only have guessed at. But, as I've noted, the terrestrial is also celestial, inasmuch as we're on a whizzing planet whose solar system drifts in a wheeling galaxy, which itself drifts in a local galaxy cluster amid billions of galaxies.

And so on, *ad infinitum?* Very possibly yes.

I wish I knew if the cosmos really is infinite. It would add a touch of surreality to my résumé: that of a star-processed, sun-begotten, two-footed, slightly arrhythmic heartbeat wondering where and what kind of place this is. All the while, I'm, therefore, daily aware that every least little thing—from my morning coffee to Groucho's cigar—is cosmic.

ADAM'S NEEDFUL NAVEL

ONCE UPON A not so very long ago, to claim that this world existed epochs before humans ever showed up was damnable. People were burnt alive for less. Centuries passed, the burnings stopped, but Earth's true age remained unguessed.

A good many men and women of Victorian England, being *de facto* Creationists, strenuously denied the temporal depth of the world which Darwinian evolution implied. Biblical authority assured them God created Earth expressly for humankind. The sequence of creation in the Book of Genesis also assured them that it and people were virtual contemporaries.

Furthermore, an Earth so many orders of magnitude older than hitherto imagined would demean human dignity to a scandalous degree, lead to rampant immorality, and—as England's conservative thinkers saw it—threaten all they held dear. Darwin himself had admitted his theory on what he called "the mystery of mysteries," speciation, required an Earth older than anyone knew; and he knew only too well the young-Earth of Anglican tradition and biblical orthodoxy didn't supply them. Earth's age, therefore, became a topic almost too hot to handle.[1]

At issue were—and still are—the Big Questions, including the question of place: Where are we? Is this a world whose species were forever fixed by the Creator? Or a world in which we and the planet itself are evolving? If the latter, what does such a where imply? A world far more ancient than humans? Or one nearly as young as they?

Curiously enough, if English antagonists of Darwin's worldview had stood for ten minutes gazing panoramically out over parts of America's red-rock West, their inner content might have been altered by that context. Provided they were open-minded, they could have seen epochs of stone time ever so slowly eroding landforms all about them. They'd have seen that a young-Earth geology, so dependent on theories of "catastrophism" and "inundation" to explain Earth's look and age in ways agreeably biblical, was untenable. Southern Utah's buttes and canyons clearly imply the incomparably slower rates of change caused by the "denudation" and "fluvialism" of wind and water.

No less an authority than Sir Archibald Geikie (1835–1924), who by the 1880s was the doyen of British geology, visited the West's canyon country in 1879 and saw for himself: "Had the birthplace of geology lain on the west side of the Rocky Mountains, this [catastrophism] controversy would never have arisen. The efficacy of denudation, instead of evoking doubt, discussion, or denial, would have been one of the first principles of the science. . . ."[2] So much for "inundation" by Noah's flood.

On a breezy day, Utah's tourist magnet, Arches National Park, can furnish a see-for-yourself experience like that of Geikie. If you visit the form called Delicate Arch, be sure to wear sun glasses, though I find ski goggles even better at shielding the eyes from microscopic grains of windblown sand.

You won't see but feel them—stinging your face and hands like gusts of invisible bees. There the hugely photogenic feature called Delicate Arch easily dwarfs walkers seeking shade or shelter at its base, whose parabola of Entrada sandstone shows unforgettably what wind and water can do, if given time enough. You'll feel as much on your skin. Yet the stinging grains too small to see have done only some of the work. That ponderous and lofty arch has been brought to its present form mostly by sky water dissolving the cement which binds all sandstone, thus releasing ever more granules to blow as the wind listeth. "Little causes, long continued." They're why so much of Utah now looks like a wind church.

᛭

As for Darwin, who was socially well-connected and born to privilege, his famous delay in publishing what he knew to be true about speciation arose from a very real fear of being thought a traitor to his class. He confided as much to a friend when he said that finally publishing *On the Origin of Species* had felt "like confessing a murder." England's establishment tended to agree. The Church of England officially damned evolution as "false, foul, French, atheistic, materialistic, and immoral."[3] On the other hand, the geologists kept turning up evidence favoring Darwin's work. And that further bugged his Victorian critics.

Before laughing at benighted Brits, who 150 years ago recoiled from evolution as amoral and godless, we should remember that poll after poll reveals the majority of Americans still incline in that direction, just as a majority of Americans struggle to locate their home state on a map.

Though no Anglican, Philip Gosse (1810–1888) was a Creationist embodying with remarkable clarity two worldviews which polarized England's chattering classes: the sacred and the scientific. As a biologist, his research was admired by competent judges, including Darwin. Nor was Gosse alone in wrestling to reconcile biblical fundamentalism with his studies of marine life and minuscule sea creatures. In those days, Anglican orthodoxy permeated English science, especially geology. Gosse, therefore, personifies orthodoxy's fear of being where and what we are: evolved creatures in an evolving universe.

On the one hand, he was a reputable scientist; on the other, a lay preacher who headed a tiny congregation of Plymouth Brethren, doing so with a literalist faith in scripture which verged on obsession. Yet his knowledge of small-scale marine fauna was so respected that, two years before publishing *On the Origin of Species,* Darwin's friend and fellow scientist Joseph Hooker (1817–1911) went round to sound out Gosse. Which side would he be on when the storm broke?

In his classic memoir *Father and Son* (1907), Edmund Gosse recalled his parent's reaction to that dilemma: "Every instinct in his intelligence went out at first to greet the new light" with its geological proofs of fossilized avatars.[4] After all, the man had spent years analyzing tidal pools and their tiny creatures. The other side of his mind, however, was rigid as the stone tablets supposedly given Moses. Biblical authority remained unquestionable. Or did it? His own meticulous field work and hours at the microscopic told him Darwin must surely be right. Species aren't static; they evolve.

But Darwin right and the *Bible* wrong? Impossible! His divided brain was that of a dedicated scientist who, at the same time, took the Book of Genesis quite literally. That split caused Edmund Gosse to open *Fathers and Sons* with a poignantly telling comment on the difference between him and his dad: "This book is the record of a struggle between two temperaments, two consciences and almost two epochs. . . . Of the two human beings here described, one was born to fly backward, the other could not help being carried forward."[5] A century and a half later, retrogressive minds are still flying backward. Nor do they see the irony in their fallible brains proclaiming the *Bible* infallible.

As Edmund Gosse tells us, his father's mind became the site of a war between its religious lobe and scientific lobe, to a degree which almost deranged the poor man. At last, however, his Good Angel won out. (Or was it his Bad Angel?) Despite what he knew scientifically, Gosse resolved to reject evolution and "to hold steadily to the law of the fixity of species," thus to his fundamentalist reading of Genesis.[6] But how, then, should he view those pesky fossils so un-biblically ancient-seeming?

With what he must have supposed was divine enlightenment, he devised and published—sincerely if foolishly—one of the most pathetic evasions this side of Lysenko or Intelligent Design. Proudly, Gosse announced his *trouvé* in a book titled *Omphalos* (1857), Greek for "navel."

Why the odd title? It referred to a classic controversy over Adam's own navel. Had he one? After all, Adam hadn't a mom. So, lacking any umbilical connection, you'd think the Creator would not have equipped his handmade human with a belly button. "Not so!" said Gosse. Adam did, too, have a navel.

But why? What on Earth for?

When we open that sealed envelope, we find the elder Gosse has unwittingly re-invented "Urban's argument." Pope Urban VIII (1568–1644), using a concept attributed to him, though never authenticated as his, refuted Galileo's case for the diurnal and orbital motions of Earth—similarly in conflict with scriptural literalism—by claiming our planet doesn't actually revolve and circle the sun; God just gave things the *appearance* that it does. So, too, in explaining away long, un-biblical reaches of geologic time as implied by fossilized species, *Omphalos* gave Adam a belly button.

"Yes," said Gosse, "those fossils *do* seem to refute Genesis. But only *seem* to." Actually, the Almighty did indeed create this world in the *Bible's* stipulated six days. "There had been no gradual modification of the surface of the earth, or slow development of organic forms." Instead God had created it "instantly, with structural *appearance* of a planet on which life has long existed."[7] Complete with Adam's belly button? By all means. Adam had one for the same reason rocks have those bothersome fossils—to save the appearances.

Thus spake *Omphalos.* No book was ever published, says his son, "with greater anticipations of success." Philip Gosse was sure it would end the Darwinian controversy by soothing atheists and Christians alike. It would, therefore, "fling geology into the arms of Scripture." He wished.

Omphalos quickly made him a laughing stock, just as two centuries before "Urban's argument" had spurred Rome's satirical wits into cracking wise. Instead of the acclaim that Gosse had prepared to revel in, he was hissed and derided by both camps. Darwinians viewed him as a turncoat, whereas devout believers angrily reviled Gosse for making the Lord out to be a whopping geological liar who had salted fake strata with phony fossils.

Thereafter, the man's spirit deflated like fallen soufflé. He withdrew from his customary attendance at scientific meetings, ceased meddling with large views, and narrowed his gaze to the eyepiece of his microscope, presumably trying not to see what he saw, so as to see only what he believed, thereby not to be what and where he was.

During backpacks down in the Grand Canyon, I've pondered rock acres of fossils embedded in great limestone wrecks and chunks that once tumbled thousands of feet down from the Kaibab stratum on the rim. And I've smiled at their relation to Adam's belly button.

The coincidence of my encountering elsewhere a young grad student whom I'll call Jason offers a twenty-first century parallel to Philip Gosse. His go-between emails had been instrumental in setting up my debate with the Creationist Binford Pyle, but till the night of that event I'd met Jason only electronically.

Then, just before the debate's moderator began tapping the microphone for a sound check, a tall, gangly fellow came up to me and put forth his hand, "You're Reg Saner, aren't you? I'm Jason. Thanks for coming." Though I liked him on sight, our brief chat still has me dumbfounded. I learned that, while working on his advanced degree in astrobiology at the University of Colorado, he was somehow managing to retain his belief in Creationism!

Taken aback, I blurted an incredulous, "But how can you? Astrobiology depends utterly and entirely on evolution. I don't get it. Isn't it hard?"

He quietly admitted, "Well . . . yes, it can be."

His tone, however, conveyed no hint of inner conflict or even difficulty, just inconvenience. Then a tactful nod from the moderator cued me to take my place on the speaker's platform, so I hadn't time to ply Jason further. Nor did he seem much inclined to be quizzed. Consequently, all I can say is that Philip Gosse lives. And not only in Jason.

Resembling Philip Gosse's dilemma even more closely, there's the recent case of Kurt Wise, a Creationist paleontologist who at Harvard studied under no less a mentor than Stephen Jay Gould. In a *New York Times Magazine* article (27 November 2007), Hanna Rosin quotes Wise as saying, "If all the evidence in the universe turned against creationism, I would be the first to admit it, but I would still be a Creationist because that is what the Word of God seems to indicate. Here I must stand."

Wise's faithful belief in the unbelievable feels oddly admirable in its staunch way. Yet how distant is it from the unshakable certitude of the suicide bomber who believes indiscriminate death and mutilation are what Allah wants and will reward?

Hutton, called by an admirer "the man who invented time," was a deist who certainly believed in a Creator but ruefully predicted that Earth's true age would produce culture shock: "It is not any part of the process that will be disputed; but after allowing all the parts, the whole will be denied; and for what?—only because we are not disposed to allow that quantity of time which the ablution of so much wasted mountain might require."[4]

Time's quantity? Even today, to use Kirwan's word, we "recoil." Tourists arriving at the Grand Canyon—whether from Chicago or Cairo, London or Berlin, Beijing or Tokyo, Caracas or São Paolo—do just that. They gaze into its depths and feel themselves missing from our own planet.

"Recoil?" says every Grand Canyon pebble, "How very naive."

Yes, egoism is indeed a form of naiveté. Our ephemerality and self-importance take a lot of reconciling.

In an earlier chapter, I claimed the natural world—the only world there is—confronts us adults with much we prefer not to think about. An incident, in of all places Italy, illustrates that sort of denial. Beginning my stay as an invited guest of the Rockefeller Foundation at its Villa Serbelloni on Lake Como, I sat down to my first lunch as the only newcomer at the table. The others, having been in residence weeks before my arrival, naturally asked what sort of writing I did. I mentioned that Grand Canyon piece, just finished, and explained my fascination with its topic. Instantly, the person on my right crudely dismissed geological time with, "Who gives a shit?"

Looking him in the eye, I said, "Obviously, you do."

That put him off balance. In a defensive tone, he asked, "What makes you think that?'

"Geological time threatens the ego. People say it's boring because of the unflattering implications." Guests who had been made to feel the extent of his conceit later told me my riposte had scored a bull's-eye.

The Grand Canyon's erosional cathedral of "terrain features" evoked from its earliest Anglo explorers a swarm of high-sounding names. Within a dozen or so miles of its winding length, your binoculars can scope out Zoroaster Temple, Brahma Temple, Horus Temple, Osiris Temple, Buddha Temple, Buddha Cloister, and Confucius Temple. Sacred places often disguise their powers, and the truly sacral has nothing to do with niceness. Nor is it bound to speak comfortably.

One midday, while backpacking along the Tonto Plateau deep within the Grand Canyon, I took refuge from the Arizona sun in a skimpy patch of shade and stayed there for much of the afternoon. All about me I saw nothing deific, just gray-green alluvial fans dustier than elephant toes, with sparse yucca and beaver-tail cactus punctuating sandy soil punctuated by lithic scatter. Beyond its lizard-flicked rubble were vistas of rust strata and rock-walled distance, mindless and wonderful. Even in the blast-furnace heat I valued wholeheartedly my simply being there.

Despite the immense quiet, despite its 2,500 years of almost continual habitation by Indians and ongoing Hopi ritual, I knew the canyon's spectacular beauty to have been created by the chance intersection of horizontal force with vertical force, of gravity with the snake-like twist and drive of wind and water across the Colorado Plateau and in the Colorado River. Temples? Their layers of limestone and shale had been granulated into shape through the down-falling rain and gravity's tireless pull, which set cliff bits to plunging and tumbling. Nature's blind building up to throw down.

During that torrid afternoon, subdued to a half-trance by an Arizona sun which felt equatorial, I did what for me is the one thing most difficult: nothing whatever. My restlessness is all the more irrational, because I know perfectly well that doing nothing has centered some of the most precious moments of my life.

So there I sat, scrunching to my left every now and then just to stay in the shadow of a fallen crag of Kaibab limestone while watching the largest bees I've ever seen, as they fumbled at pollen amid flowering stalks of agave. Near Redwall boulders chock full of fossilized crinoids, corals, bryozoans, they drowsily carried on their lives as social insects while gathering pollen over trilobites whose habits, unknowable, survive only in seas of solid limestone. Dropping from bloom to bloom they flew heavily, as if their fuzzy black bodies were too big for their wings and those agave blossoms all but too rich for them.

After the last bee had bumbled off and away, I turned to watch canyon ravens ride thermals high above other fossil-rich chunks of that blocky limestone—atop which, sporadically, collared lizards did sets of those brisk little pushups they're given to, with me lazily wondering why. Desert rain, resurrected into nearby clumps of beaver-tail cactus, made a frugal contrast with the prodigal rush and surge of the Colorado River some 700 feet below, through what's called the Inner Gorge. Depending on breeze, its voice swelled to suggest the river's muscular power, then waned to a whisper, then again rose. Aware that the same river had spoken throughout canyon-carving eons, I gave my permission: "No need to mind me. Just say whatever you said long before this, when there was no one to hear it."

So, under cliffs like ripened enigmas, I river-listened. On and off all afternoon, I heard—in the hustle, then roar, then hush—the sound of the world falling forever away from the world and the river's voice, pouring, pouring . . . through everything we believe.

ARIAS AND ATOM BOMBS

IN EURIPIDES'S late play, *The Bacchae*, a god, Dionysus, tells the headstrong Pentheus, "You do not know what your life is—nor what you are doing, nor who you are." It humbles one that words written some 2,400 years ago continue to describe us, from Stephen Hawking to you and me and Paris Hilton. (Note the crescendo effect.)

At the risk of tediousness, I repeat once again that all serious writing is both a form of discovery and a mode of self-creation. In my case, woefully imperfect, of course. No, make that hyper-woefully, although, thanks to my kind of creationism, I'm now a tad more insightful than my earlier versions. Such self-evolving can happen because—to extend Werner Heisenberg's famous dictum—the act of observation alters not only the what's observed, but the observer as well.

In fact, by dint of just looking around this world right under my nose and making *written* observations, I've been altered enough to become almost infinitely ignorant. Which I rather enjoy. It has the feel of an achievement. After all, there's positive ignorance and negative ignorance. Socrates's kind was positive. He knew that, compared to the possibilities, he knew little; however, if your ignorance is the negative kind, you don't know you don't know. Thus, enlarging your positive ignorance to just this side of infinity calls for some inkling as to how many creatures, things, and interactions there are for you to be ignorant of. Your advantage over the cocksure but clue-less Pentheus comes of knowing at least that much.

And a little more, since going forth to see for yourself enhances you in ways mediated knowledge can never equal. Add to that the mental energy required for making those written observations as thoughtfully as your temperament allows and you've entered the self-creative mode. A spoil-sport might say, "This thing you call your idea of creationism . . . why, it's nothing but education!"

To which I would say, blushingly, "Well, yes, a kind of self-educational evolving. But how bad is that?"

Surely, it can't be true that my observations put into writing have altered me more than all the rest of my experiences combined. Surely, it only feels that way. But that is indeed, though very roughly, the feeling—and with some basis in fact. Our lived experience relived via language acquires more depth and permanence than it could ever retain if we hadn't put it into written words. Which, in turn, become part of who we are. Yet it's important to note that "lived experience" includes going forth to see for yourself. As, for example, when writing and related "going forth" re-shaped my relation to the atom bomb.

So, as to see for myself, I drove miles of winding gravel road way up the valley of a stream called the Pecos just to lay eyes on Robert Oppenheimer's cabin in the Jemez Mountains about an hour's drive west of Santa Fe. It sat in a high meadow whose wildflowers sloped eagerly up to the porch, and it had a magnificent westward view of summits and their snowfields. He always liked a view. Back in 1929, writing from Berkeley to his brother, Frank, he mentioned often visiting "some boys who have . . . a beautiful cabin on the hill, with a view and great stone fireplace and balconies and so on." For Oppenheimer there was ever and always the aesthetic dimension.

As to the Bomb, my teenage attitudes had been saturated with years of anti-Japanese propaganda and media coverage. Like Pentheus in Euripides's play, I knew my country was justified in dropping a thousand such bombs on Japan. "After all," I told myself, "they started it." Though I'd never seen a Japanese, I knew those dirty Japs deserved whatever they got. What I didn't know was the appalling extent of my ignorance and inhumanity. Two decades later, a visit to New Mexico's Pajarito Plateau set me writing pages that enlightened me on more than details of nuclear fission.

Among much else, I learned, for example, that, long before Los Alamos and the Bomb, Robert Oppenheimer had confided to a friend, "My two great loves are physics and New Mexico. It's a pity they can't be combined."[1] The fact that an appreciative response to the beauty of northern New Mexico had helped level Hiroshima and Nagasaki revealed the cooperative/predatory duality of human nature as dramatically as any example I'm aware of. The best way to produce collaborative interaction in a group is to point out an enemy called "they," who threatens a group called "us." Apropos of that technique, note the parallel with Creationists who energize collaboration among "us godly ones" by claiming "they" (the evolutionary scientists) threaten "our morals, our values, and our children's very souls." As to our species' predatory side, Creationism says it comes of Original Sin and God's punishment for that transgression, whereas the deadly hateful "Darwinism" says it evolved naturally.

My essay, "Technically Sweet," began, simply enough, with a mental image. On New Mexico's Pajarito Plateau, I pictured an actual atom bomb atop human footprints in the plateau's dusty soil, once inhabited by those ancestral Pueblo people we call the Anasazi. Stone age, atomic age—simple and stark. But much less simple than I thought.

Writing the essay soon led me to facets I hadn't dreamed of. For example, the aesthetic and the sexual. Because the sexual factor is largely inferential, I'll comment on the other aspect first. At this distance in time, we think our wartime success in making the atom bomb was inevitable. Not so. The whole project might have flopped. Ironically, two big reasons it didn't were Robert Oppenheimer and the aesthetic influence exerted by "the enchanted land" of northern New Mexico.

The skinny, gawky, teenage Robert Oppenheimer had been shipped westward from New York City by parents hoping the change might benefit his health and bring him out of his nerdy shell. But that isn't why Los Alamos was the site chosen for bomb-making. The adult Oppenheimer was, first and foremost, a scientist, open to considering several other locations. Yet, eventually, the fact that his adolescent self had been delighted with northern New Mexico turned out to be crucial. What had charmed him could charm the scientists brought to work behind barbed wire in carefully guarded isolation.

Emilio Segrè—bosom buddy of Enrico Fermi both in their native Rome and at Los Alamos and later a Nobel laureate himself—attributed to the Jemez Mountains, their "cloudscapes," their profusion of wildflowers blooming through long New Mexican summers, as well as the hiking trails and trout streams and ski slopes and Pueblo ruins and mineral beds "a decisive part in sustaining the great effort," making the Bomb.[2]

Not only that. He went out of his way to *emphasize* the influence of place: "Often at the end of a strenuous period of work, one felt completely exhausted, but the out-of-doors was always a source of renewed strength."[3] Fermi's wife, Laura, called it "the most spectacular country I had ever seen."[4] Niels Bohr was entranced. Typically, Richard Feynman called it "sensational." And those reactions were fairly unanimous among the wives and scientists there at the time.

In backpacking over the once-sacred home of ancestral Pueblo peoples called the Anasazi, now dominated by the laboratories of Los Alamos, I came across hundreds of obsidian flakes chipped away centuries ago in making arrowheads and scrapers. There was a similar scattering of old potsherds on the same dusty clay soil. After pitching my tent, I enjoyed the desert evening's last glimmers while roaming among those ancient relics lying clustered by the dozen. Taken together, obsidian's keen, cutting edge and a dull clay potsherd began feeling like opposites different as wounds and food, killing and nurture, war and peace. Yet they were also examples of human creativity; thus, not so opposite after all. Their interrelation begot, therefore, a slight ambiguity. Soon, even the line between me, peacenik, and Oppenheimer began to blur, as did other, ancillary oppositions along with it.

Although prior to writing "Technically Sweet" I'd have said I was innocent of any connection to the Bomb, my innocence soon grew problematic. In retrospect, for instance, I relived mixed feelings during a stopover at Hiroshima on my way to the fighting in Korea, where, as an infantry platoon leader, my "duty" involved killing more Asians.

On that New Mexican plateau, therefore, many antitheses blurred into each other. Among them the sexual. For me pots have always seemed womb-like, partly because women make pots, so an association with the womb unconsciously begot another enclosure and birth motif.

As I delved books on Oppenheimer and the Bomb, further factual details of enclosure began to emerge, some suggesting a weird relation between sexuality and the Bomb. For example, at summer camp the fourteen-year-old Oppenheimer was set upon by boys who painted his private parts green. They then kept his humiliated sex organs and the enraged, humiliated rest of him cooling all night by locking him up in the camp's ice house.

Think about that for a moment. Suppose that, when you were fourteen, derided as a sissified and brain proud geek, the other kids ganged up on you. Suppose they held you down while somebody slathered green paint on your groin and privates. Imagine what might being going through your head all night.

My essay's final draft opened with that adolescent prank, asking, "What, however distantly, might such a boyhood trauma have caused to happen?"

Further along, the piece recounted a curiously ironic detail. At Los Alamos, fissionable material (radioactively "hot" and, thus, metaphorically angry) had been stored in an ice house. In a sense, that earlier ice house, which had once imprisoned the humiliated boy, certainly contained an incipient explosion. Images of womblike enclosure also included the first A-bomb inflicted on humans, dubbed "Little Boy." What's more, it had been dropped from the *belly* of a Superfort, the Enola Gay, a "womb" complete with female name. But not the name of just any female. Enola Gay was the pilot's own mother. True, coincidence happens. Even so. . . .

In the mix, I learned, was also a case of puppy love. One of Oppenheimer's biographers claimed that the teenage Robert had, during his magical summers in

New Mexico, come under the spell of Katherine Page, recently married but still "a fascinating and romantic figure."[5] Another biographer claimed the eighteen-year-old was "infatuated" and "adoring" of this comely and—by numerous accounts—undeniably vital young woman. He and a male age-mate were smitten enough to be known as Katherine's "slaves." In a letter to his brother, Frank, the adult Oppenheimer even mentioned having had a nocturnal dream which featured her attractive self and person.[6]

Freudianism is now out of fashion, yet no well-informed person doubts the power of the unconscious. Among more obvious factors, I began wondering to what extent the Bomb site and the Bomb were influenced by motives the scientific director of the Manhattan Project was wholly unaware of. As for that, how many of us truly know what we're doing and why?

As to the role played by his sense of beauty, Oppenheimer was repeatedly asked why he lent his genius to such a destructive enterprise. He gave many answers but perhaps came closest to the truth when he admitted that for a physicist the solution to the problem was "technically sweet."

For him, as I've noted, the aesthetic dimension was never trivial. During the highly charged evening before the Trinity shot, he had looked to the low range of the adjacent Oscura Mountains, just as dusk was blurring their ridgelines under a darkening sky, and remarked to a fellow scientist, "Funny how the mountains always inspire our work."[7]

As mentioned above, Creationists explain the *chiaroscuro* of human nature by resorting to Original Sin and the Fall from grace of our first parents. I agree, except that I locate humankind's original sin somewhere in the lost history of our evolution. Not every species of primate engages in violence and predation. Somewhere—way back when—perhaps our avatars could have evolved more peaceably but took a wrong turn we're all paying for. However that may be, my kind of creationism convinces me that coping with our dark side would profit from less insistence on our sinful nature and better knowledge of the evolutionary past still alive in our present selves.

The paradox so conspicuous in that fruitful cooperation which produced our species' most destructive tool is differently illustrated by a pleasant summer evening of musical art.

Imagine yourself in the audience—many of them tourists—on opening night at the Santa Fe Opera's very first production: July 3rd, 1957. For its premier event the company has chosen Puccini's *Madam Butterfly*. But, because it's an outdoor theater, sunset's afterglow to the northwest complicates the experience as do, through clear desert air, city lights twinkling thirty miles away.

Meanwhile, on stage, the plaintive Cho-cho san longs for a first glimpse of Pinkerton's returning ship and sings her hopeful aria, *Un bel dì*. How many listeners in the audience realize that those distant lights are Los Alamos? How many recall that Cho-cho san's love story takes place in Nagasaki? The A-Bomb called Fat Man which carbonized the people of Nagasaki was built on that very Pajarito Plateau whose lights twinkle as she sings.

Could any juxtaposition of extremes be more expressive of human duality than that one? Neither it nor examples previously cited would have become part of my blood and bones and, thus, part of the talking animal I am if not for my lower-case kind of creationism.

I hadn't yet written the final page of "Technically Sweet" when, while hiking along a trail not far from my house, I paused atop Dakota Ridge. In so doing, I chanced upon an actual scene which seemed just right for concluding the essay. Nearby in the foreground, a mother held her baby as he sucked apple juice from his bottle, while seven miles away I could clearly see the plutonium "trigger" factory called Rocky Flats. Their strikingly visual antithesis begot these closing words: "We must be better than we are. That, too, is our nature."

JOURNEY TO THE CENTER PLACE

PUEBLO PEOPLES of the Southwest hold to the tradition of their evolution, which they call the Emergence. Up from some watery underworld, supporting their fishlike or embryonic state, they rose by degrees to their present bipedal forms, paralleled by their gradual rise from low behavior to rectitude. Though this Emergence myth offers an explanation very different from those often given to "Mommy, where did I come from?" the shared impulse toward where, why, when, and how is similar. A human embryo, after all, even looks like a sort of tadpole.

Pueblo variants of this sunless underworld from which pre-human beings issued don't greatly differ. A Zuñi version, for instance, gives these pre-human forebears the long tails, scaly skins, with the webbed fingers and toes of muddy creatures whose bulging, owlish eyes blinked constantly. At Acoma Pueblo, the stories feature beings with squishy bodies only half-finished. Hopi myth, in contrast, dwells on furry-coated, doglike critters with mixed traits of coyotes and bears, though with webbed fingers and lizard tails. Their confused bodies matched their behavior, which was confusedly violent, sexually chaotic, and even given to cannibalism. Emergence from this lawless, underworld state was followed by an indefinitely long phase of wanderings and migrations. And the goal? To find at last their rightful place—the center place—while developing more fully evolved bodies and a way of going more upright than reptilian.

Unmistakably, these ancient explanations tell of bodily and behavioral developments unfolding together. It's impossible not to think how closely their stories match the biological maxim: ontogeny recapitulates phylogeny. Your passage and mine from embryo to fetal creature with a tail in a dark and watery place, to the quadrupedal gait of a crawling infant following no law but appetite, to bipedal adult made each of us a one-person enactment of humanity's physical and moral evolution. (Do Creationists ever speak of the tail bone?)

The fact that some tribes of the Southwest claim their Emergence occurred from or near the Grand Canyon has struck me as a pleasant coincidence. I, too, in emerging from the same place on a particular afternoon, experienced something of the sort. I wasn't born again, as in moving to Colorado, just born deeper. Unless you yourself are made of stone, you cannot spend day after day rambling half a billion years down in gone time, scrambling about within its lithic abyss, and not be altered.

Instead of finding a physical "center place," however, my emergence occasioned no blinding flash, no mystic vision or revelation. Between the trekking, the note-taking, the long thought that goes into written language, it simply led me to *know* my place better. Unforgettably so, as it happens.

To particularize what the ascent upward meant to me, I must quote a passage not in the Grand Canyon piece I've been referring to but a related one:

"As if I were climbing the ladder up and out from a kiva's dusk into sunlight—which among living Pueblos is a symbolic repetition of the Emergence myth—my ascent from the Colorado River took me from my past life as blue-green algae, then trilobite, then crinoid, then reptile, then rat, then ape, then *Homo erectus* . . . till finally I climbed out onto the South Rim of now.

"It was a rise whose stages were written in stone; from the Inner Gorge of Vishnu Schist, up past Zoroaster Granite onto Tapeats Sandstone, over the broad Tonto Plateau and up again, past Bright Angel Shale, Muav Limestone, Redwall Limestone, upward still through the complex Watahomigi Formation, the Manakacha, the Wescogame, then rising through Esplanade Sandstone, hermit Shale, Coconino Sandstone, the Toroweap Formation, with the final few yet strenuous hundreds of feet up through and out onto Kaibab limestone."

Deep experiences take a while to sink in. Slowly, over a year and more, my little personal Emergence, written, began altering my view of things and people. That's creationism for you, and this slow dawning of heightened awareness is historically true for our species as a whole. On the individual level, however, the stark reality of our human situation is for many intolerable. Not distasteful, unpleasant, ugly, repellent. Intolerable. That which cannot be faced must be denied. But how? By staying well inside Plato's cave.

In his great dialogue, *The Republic,* written 2,500 years ago, Plato described a dim cave where people sit chained lifelong in such a way that their heads must fixedly stare away from light at the cave's mouth. They can observe only the cave's back wall, where a shadow-play is presented by puppet-like semblances of human figures and objects being carried past outside. Since those umbral flickers thrown against the cave's back wall are all they know of the external world, they mistake them for reality itself. Had they ventured forth, their eyes would at first have been overwhelmed by the world's fully sunlit actualities. But, if an escapee from the cave, after acclimating to sunlight and seeing the real world, should return to his chained fellows and report on the falsity of those deceptive shadows, they would either declare him mad or kill him. "Human kind cannot bear very much reality," wrote the poet T. S. Eliot in a line clearly echoing Plato.[1]

From early childhood my cave walls were dogmas truer than granite. People I trusted above all others told me that to doubt our dogmas' shadow version of the world is a grievous offense against God, who loves me to pieces. Worse yet, if I should dare to go outside and stay there, He would send my immortal soul to hell for all eternity. Because my nearest and dearest clearly believed what they said, I did, too. Naturally, we didn't think it a cave. Instead, we called it the one true Church, as instructed.

Although Plato lived more than two millennia ago, nothing has changed. For the mind's eye of many, perhaps most, leaving that comfortably muted cave light and its shadows to face the solar glare outside is more than they can take. But what of superior me? Had I risen up in the cave, denounced its shadow-play world, and flung heroically forth into the light? Nothing so grandly dramatic. Kneeling at mass one day I simply asked myself, "Do you really believe all this?"

The matter-of-fact reply surprised me. "Actually, no. I don't." And that was that. Didn't believe it and couldn't. The organ chords, the smoking incense, the hymns and hosannas had been my virtual home, but they were wafting upward toward a deity compounded of contradictions. At some indefinable point, my rock-solid belief began eroding toward only believing I believed. So no hero points for me. As for my fall into knowledge, sixteen years of Catholic education were to blame. Nuns whose memory I still cherish and priests I still respect set the highest value on truth and taught me that I should always obey my conscience. So I did and left the cave.

Yet, when among sincere and uncombative believers, I avoid tampering. If their doctrines aren't harmful to others, and if they add reassurance to life, why undermine them? Reality isn't for everyone, nor even for me, unceasingly. It can be dangerous in ways which give some validity to the saying, "Where ignorance is bliss 'tis folly to be wise." Stark naked reality can make you feel equally naked and vulnerable. In truth, whether life be absurd, incomparably worth living, or "a cosmic joke" is far less a question of intellect than of temperament. Oh, I, too, love a good show, and Catholicism puts on one of the oldest and best, a show which part of my heart fondly recalls. Nonetheless, I prefer the natural magic of this world. Perhaps that's why my writing began with poetry. However fantastic a poem's apparent subject may seem, its true subject is about the way things really are.

The irony of anti-evolutionists denying the truth of our animal heritage is that it amounts to devolving, taking a downward path rather than an upward one; whereas, for us talking mammals, knowledge is the center place.

PINOCCHIO'S NOSE

NO SENSIBLE PERSON denies the daily consolation and strength which genuinely religious faith gives countless millions of decent people. Nor would such a person deride honest piety in anyone. Quite apart from issues of truth or theological validity, the evolved survival value of religion is self-evident. It promotes group solidarity, offers solace to grief, and gives meaning to a world which may frequently appear incoherent, even chaotic. Although much religious participation consists of only going through the motions, that solace and the social benefits of church-going remain verifiable.

As stated at the outset of this book, what I deplore in the attempts by Creationist leaders to subvert the "establishment clause" of the U.S. Constitution is their resort to immoral methods in the name of morality. Doing evil that good may come of it corrupts the very soul of true religion.

As to evil deeds, I favor Socrates's view that they represent a failure of knowledge. Perhaps that's why, over half a lifetime, I have vividly remembered a black man who stood speechifying in a public plaza off Chicago's Michigan Avenue. My friend Red Grisetto called the place Bughouse Square. "It's where all the crackpots go to yak at anybody who'll listen."

At a nearby bench, I had plumped down to eat lunch on the cheap—a whole-wheat bagel with cream cheese—when the man's tone caught my attention. Of the half dozen or more other speakers scattered around the plaza, he was the only one Red might not have called a "nut."

Shabby, gray-haired, he seemed perhaps fifty, fifty-five, wore a baggy tweed suit-coat that didn't match his pants, and had stuffed one pocket with what looked like leftovers from his own lunch. Yet behind wire-rimmed glasses the brown eyes shone with intelligence, and his manner seemed that of a schoolmaster addressing children for whom difficult things must be kept very, very simple.

"Why," he oratorically asked no one in particular, "do I bother to stand here talking?" I pricked up my ears. Why indeed?

"I do it," he explained, "because ignorance will hurt me."

His defensive mission, therefore, was to enlighten. And the enlightenment—what form did it take? I've forgotten, perhaps mercifully. Yet, ever since then, I've cherished the genius of that one sentence: "Ignorance will hurt me." Never have I heard anything truer.

On December 21, 2005, in a Dover, Pennsylvania, courtroom, U.S. District Judge John E. Jones III, appointed to the bench by President George W. Bush, took a similar view of ignorance as hurtful. In his 139-page decision against a local school board's attempt to introduce Intelligent Design as an alternative to evolutionary science, he not only judged the teaching of ID to be unconstitutional, but exposed its bogus claim to be science. "The overwhelming evidence," his decision stated, "is that Intelligent Design is a religious view . . . and not a scientific theory. It is an extension of the fundamentalists' view that one must either accept the literal interpretation of Genesis or else believe in the godless system of evolution." (The word "godless," be it noted, alluded to Creationism's favorite charge against evolution.)

One of the trial lawyers arguing the case against ID had referred specifically to the hurtfulness of ignorance: "At a time when this country is lagging behind other countries, we can ill afford to shackle our children's minds with 15th century science."[1]

As is well known, organized religion's grudging mistrust of scientific advances can be extreme. Darwin himself pointed out that—incredible as it may seem today—Newton's law of gravity was attacked by the great philosopher Gottfried Wilhelm Leibnitz (1646–1716) "as subversive of natural, and inferentially revealed, religion."[2] Gravity irreligious? Even so fine a thinker as Leibnitz wasn't immune to mental inertia.

My own animus against Creationism springs not only from its missionary zeal in spreading darkness. The narrative that Darwinian evolution tells is the most wonderful story I know and all the more marvelous for being true. That Creationism should deceive generations of youngsters into thinking Darwin evil and evolution a conspiracy is like pouring ink into the sun.

Requiring biology teachers to tiptoe past evolution makes as much sense as reading words of a great narrative in alphabetical order. Not only that. The political party most cozy with fundamentalism and the Religious Right has done irreparable damage to this planet by jackhammering our environmental safeguards. Granted, we can't do without industry, but what can we do without a livable planet?

Sadly, mendacity for Christ seems the Creationist way. To a list of whoppers it adds slander of the living and the dead. If forced to abandon their policy of bearing false witness, Creationists leaders, new style and old, would be struck dumb.

Principal among these many deceits aimed at hoodwinking the public is the lie that evolution is controversial, even in crisis. The 2,000 scientist members of the National Academy of Sciences, including 160 Nobel laureates, affirm the *fact* of evolution. In an official statement, the National Association of Biology Teachers, numbering some 8,000 members, doesn't mince words: "Nothing in biology makes sense except in the light of evolution."[3] Depending on their audience, speakers on behalf of Intelligent Design (ID) often say or imply that Darwinian evolution attributes everything to chance, whereas, in truth, natural selection is, in the phrase of mathematician Allen Paulos, "a highly nonrandom process."[4] Also, such speakers often imply—dishonestly—that Darwin's theory is about the origin of life. Not so. It's about changes in life forms. Another pervasive mode of deception cites, misleadingly, words taken out of context or quotes edited to mislead.

In fact, Judge Jones reprimanded members of the Dover school board for lying under oath.

Prior to the Dover case, and by way of reclaiming America for Christ, one Phillip Johnson, a lawyer and deep thinker of the Intelligent Design brain trust, devised a strategy for defying the Constitution's "establishment clause," separating church and state. To begin the moral regeneration of America, his sect would infiltrate school curricula. The fact that old-style Creationism had become a talk-show joke proved you couldn't gain entry to classrooms merely by thumping the *Bible*. Johnson seems, therefore, to have told himself, "It's time to don lab coats and claim we're scientists." With startling candor, his strategy was dubbed "the Wedge," and in 1998 its manifesto was formally written up by like-minded others.

That key document explained the Creationist aim of ending public education's nonsectarian character by making evolution the point of entry for the wedge-like concept of ID. Once school walls were breached, evangelical Christianity would follow.

Accordingly, to avoid blowing their scientific cover, spokesmen for ID eschew the appeals to scripture employed by old-style Creationists. Too, they generally accept modern geology's estimates on the age of our planet. Furthermore, instead of insisting on strict fidelity to the opening verses of Genesis, they concede that small changes in life-forms may be produced by evolution—but not entire species.

Darwin's theory, in contrast, predicts an unbroken transition of "descent with variation" from species to species. Mountains of evidence corroborating his prediction haven't deterred ID's advocates from trying to wedge their creed into the schools. They declare Darwinian evolution to be "in crisis," because it is scientifically flawed and—worse yet—the gateway to godlessness. So they woo school boards and citizens with apparently valid science proving only an Intelligent Designer could possibly have contrived the biological complexities which surround us. Tactfully, they leave this preternaturally intelligent cause unnamed.

That plot thickens, however, when we learn that Mr. Phillip Johnson, in speaking to his coreligionists, admitted ID's scientific pose is just that: "This isn't really, and never has been, a debate about science. . . . It's about religion and philosophy."[5] A few years later, Johnson came even cleaner at a conference titled "Reclaiming America for Christ," sponsored through the Coral Ridge Ministries founded by the same D. James Kennedy who begot the nationally aired TV documentary, *Darwin's Deadly Legacy* (2006). Addressing his fellow believers, Johnson revealed much more: "The objective is to convince people that Darwinism is inherently atheistic, thus shifting the debate from creationism vs. evolution to the existence of God vs. the nonexistence of God. From there people are introduced to the truth of the Bible and then the question of sin and finally introduced to Jesus."[6]

"But," you may say, "if godliness is the goal, what of those Christian faiths such as Unitarian Universalism having no quarrel with Darwin or evolution? Why not make it a come-all-ye by inviting Catholicism, Methodism, Episcopalianism, and similar others into the schools?" Alas, their very acceptance of evolution proves them unfit for bringing Jesus to young lives. Only *Bible*-based, Darwin-defying born-agains are to reap the harvest and bring in the sheaves. And guess what? The dream outcome is a national takeover for Christ. *Their* Christ, of course.

Johnson's candor on "shifting the debate" disappears from ID strategy when addressing the general public. References to God, the *Bible,* and to Jesus are, as I've said, then carefully eschewed, with the implicit Designer left to be inferred.

What is most disquieting in all this is the Fundamentalist devotee's certitude that he—not Jews, Catholics, Anglicans, Quakers, Mormons, Buddhists, Hindus, Muslims, or any other sort of believer—has the absolute truth. Whether in religion or politics, nothing has been more lethal that that kind of absolute certitude. Historically, when such zealots come to power, persecution and fanaticism follow. As Mr. Dooley once said, "A fanatic is a man that does what he thinks th' Lord wud do if He knew th' facts."[7]

The Wedge has by now been upgraded to what Phillip Johnson calls "the second wedge," drawing on the persuasive talents of literary people, writers, and artists.[8]

There is also the Bridge, as conceived by mathematician William Dembski, mentioned earlier in my account of the debate with Binford Pyle. A prolific writer on behalf of ID and a highly intelligent man, Dembski has published a series of books, all of which either imply or insist, by way of philosophical and mathematical arguments, that unexplained phenomena must be the work of an Intelligent Designer.

Wishing reality other than it is must be old as human nature and believing the unbelievable makes that wish come true.

To see that it does, Dembski and lawyer/philosopher Phillip Johnson, plus biologist Michael Behe, constitute the Holy Trinity of the ID brain trust, with Dembski looking forward to the day when Christ "completes" science. "My thesis," he says, "is that the disciplines find their completion in Christ and cannot be properly understood apart from Christ. . . . The point to understand here is that Christ is never an addendum to a scientific theory but always a completion."[9] Thus, Jews, such as Albert Einstein, Niels Bohr, and Richard Feynman, are capable of "incomplete" science only, not to mention all the non-Christian physicists and biologists of Japan, China, India, or, for that matter, non-Christians of any nation whatever.

As an expression of faith, Dembski's "thesis" regards him alone, and is so entirely irrelevant to science I'm sure he sincerely believes in it. Yet, when it comes to wishfulness, Michael Behe—the ID biologist who, in the flagellum of a bacterium, has discovered God's whisker—is no slouch. He has called Intelligent Design, in which his concept of Irreducible Complexity figures as a main biological principle, "so significant that it must be ranked as one of the great achievements in the history of science."[10] Moreover, its innovation rivals the discoveries "of Copernicus, Galileo, and Einstein."[11] (Inasmuch as Einstein was a Jew, he obviously worked at a disadvantage.) Finally, there's the uncomfortable fact that biologists outside the ID network—which amounts to virtually all biologists alive—regard his Irreducible Complexity as a willful denial of how highly specialized organs evolve.

Behe isn't the only ID proponent to either deny or misrepresent evolution. In an interview as recent as April 6, 2007, Phillip Johnson remarked that, if chimpanzees are so genetically similar to humans as biologists claim, "We ought to see humans occasionally being born to chimps or perhaps chimps born into human families."[12] If the reader strains at believing Johnson ever said such a thing, much less meant it, he or she would do well to consider a question raised by the host of *Larry King Live*. In interviewing Barbara Forrest, a biologist and author, King said, "All right, hold on, Dr. Forrest, your concept of how you can out-and-out turn down creationism since if evolution is true, why are there still monkeys?"[13] King's utter ignorance of the subject surely includes the scientific meaning of the word "theory," along with the requirement that a valid theory have predictive power.

As it happens, Darwin's theory of natural selection has continued to be astonishingly predictive, even in the abstruse field of today's genetic science, which he couldn't possibly have foreseen. Intelligent Design, on the other hand, is wholly impotent to predict so much as a single biological phenomenon—or even explain one. All ID can do is invoke the supernatural: "an Intelligent Designer must've done it."

Even granting that assumption, how does it bring biology closer to explaining, for example, a rise in the incidence of autism, or breast cancer, or swine flu, or antibiotic resistant TB? We may, therefore, reasonably ask, "How on Earth can Intelligent Design have bamboozled so many Americans so successfully?" The answer is one politicians have practiced for eons: *tell your listeners what they want to hear*. Another part is illustrated by Larry King's cluelessness, cited above.

Then, too, and especially among evangelicals, there's a nagging "science anxiety," a disquieting sense that cherished beliefs and the moral order are threatened by science. Ever since Galileo clashed with the Church, scientists have made religious leaders feel uneasy, and no researcher since Galileo has so scandalized evangelicals as did Darwin. Though neither the Italian nor the Englishman intended to undermine scripture, their very different discoveries happened to reveal that certain biblical passages were not literal descriptions of the natural phenomena they referred to. But, if biblical inerrancy is a cornerstone of your temple, you are—like poor Philip Gosse—forced to deny the validity of any scientific idea which seems to contradict scripture.

By way of exploiting "science anxiety" among the pious, you merely hijack a half dozen words and render them odious. You also beat the nefarious scientists at their own game by citing abstruse biochemical processes which prove your anti-Darwinian claims, all while using pseudo-science to badmouth real science. In effect, you smear skunk oil on the words "science" and "scientists," which is exactly what your audience wants you to do.

Ironically, the tactic is a product of evolution. It developed long before *Homo sapiens* came on the scene. Even today, the surest way to instill group solidarity, whether among corvids, primates or humans, is to designate certain outsiders as "the enemy."

Then there's the blue-collar mistrust of academe. The conventionally pious share that mistrust. Many also suspect that university professors, in general, and scientists, in particular, are an amoral lot who deliberately put pernicious ideas into young minds. Worse yet, universities are hot beds of Darwinians. In point of fact, however, the word "science" derives from the Latin verb *scire,* to know. Thus, a bias against science is tantamount to a bias against knowledge, against enlightenment.

Speaking of skunk oil, I've already cited Phillip Johnson's dishonest urging of ID's devotees "to convince people that Darwinism is inherently atheistic." In real science, of course, supernatural belief or disbelief is irrelevant. Darwin's *On the Origin of Species,* whose subject is natural processes, therefore, doesn't include speculation about otherworldly agency.

As Johnson realized, however, the denotation of "atheistic" has been so soaked in skunk oil it reeks of negative connotations. Jenny and John Doe startle at "atheistic" as if at a hobgoblin. They know that atheists are capable of any imaginable foulness and twice on Sundays. Till recently, for example, South Carolina accepted the fundamentalist equating of atheism with anarchy and public ruin. It, therefore, barred such monsters from public office. That disqualification has since been removed, but till its removal we must suppose each office-holding crook in South Carolina was a believer.

So, in ID's formulation, evolution is "godless," another term whose noxious cloud of connotation smothers its denotative function. Defamation by connotation has long worked for politicians and works equally well for Creationists. Their bandying of the word "Darwin" connotes more than just atheism. Packed into its two syllables lurk degeneracy and the law of the jungle. Never mind that Charles Darwin led a moral life, which ID's spokesmen are morally obliged to know. Instead, they perpetrate libelous slurs on his name.

Just as "Darwin," "Darwinism," and "evolution" have been made toxic, so have other words and phrases, including "survival of the fittest," "liberal," and "humanist." Each has been—as a distinguished biologist puts it—"sprinkled with rat poison."[14] As for "values," the Religious Right has them all and "evolutionists" none.

Niall Shanks, formerly a science teacher at East Tennessee State University but now at Wichita State University in Kansas, says some of his students do indeed fear "that studying evolution will have terrible consequences for the fate of their souls."[15] Mark Looy, a voice in the Creationist group calling itself Answers in Genesis objects to the teaching of evolution because "It creates a sense of purposelessness and hopelessness, which I think leads to things like pain, murder, and suicide."

In a speech on the floor of the House of Representatives, former Texas Congressman Tom DeLay, who ironically enough has a degree in biology, said the 1999 shooting at Columbine High School should partly be blamed on teaching the students "that they are nothing but glorified apes who are evolutionized out of some primordial soup of mud."[16] Never mind that Darwin's theory isn't about life's origin, Creationists love to imply that it is. Ken Cummings, Dean of the Graduate School within the Institute for Creation Research, decried a PBS series on evolution as having "much in common" with the 9/11 terrorist attacks. He further claimed, "America is being attacked from within through its public schools by a militant religious movement called Darwinists. . . ."[17] From his institute's foundational truths we learn, "All things in the universe were created and made by God in the six literal days of the creation week described in Genesis 1:1–2:3, and confirmed in Exodus 20:8–11."[18]

For me, the most entertaining claim from anti-Darwinians is one by Henry Morris, also of the Institute for Creation Research. His view of evolution is that "the entire monstrous complex was revealed to Nimrod at Babel and perhaps by Satan himself. . . ."[19]

Furthermore, Creationism's favorite sing-song goes like this: "Evolution's just a theory, evolution's just a theory." The fact that theory is vital to intellection sinks from view under ID's insistently noxious innuendo. But evolution is not a theory; it's a fact. Darwin's principle of natural selection is the theory. Evolution itself is a fact massively supported by evidence, and it can be observed. Natural selection is Darwin's theory on how the *fact* of evolution happens.

Why, then, is the ID scam—that "evolution's just a theory"—so readily swallowed by school board members and their voters? By way of answer, a few questions come to mind.

Just how scientifically acute are Jenny and John Doe? Isn't America the country where fifty percent of those responding to a Harris poll of 2005 *did not know* that Earth goes around the sun and takes a year to do it?[20] Isn't this also the country which, in 2004, spent $900 million and sixteen months on an investigating whether or not Iraq had weapons of mass destruction? The investigation found no evidence that it had them. Yet, by 2005, a Harris Poll found half its respondents believed the exactly the opposite. Fully half! Talk radio kills.

By the time Creationist propaganda has made "theory" sound like self-abuse, Mr. and Mrs. Doe would rather expose their youngsters to the hordes of Genghis Kahn than to "Darwinism." Then there's the fact of gaps in the fossil record. Jenny and John may or may not know that Earth annually circles the sun, but they know gaps are bad. They couldn't tell a geological column from a cemetery headstone, but gaps? Hey, gaps—whether in teeth, fence, or trouser fly—are serious. "You can't have gaps. Everybody knows that."

In reality, of course, the fossil record is superb. Not perfect, just superb. "Ah ha," John Doe nods to Jenny, "Hear that? Not perfect." Don't bother quoting the odds against squishy critters of 3.5 billion years ago surviving as fossils while being crushed under the tremendous heat and weight of strata tens of thousands of feet thick. You'll get no sympathy. A gap is a gap is a gap. As if it were an unanswerable argument against the Darwinian threat, Creationists bow down to any old fossil gap they can find. As their critics often note, they positively worship "the God of the gaps."

Furthermore, there's the assertion that, if evolution's true, each of us humans becomes a pile of compost, a slimy dump of mere organic matter. Looking at the evolutionists I know personally, you'd never guess it. They deftly conceal the sludgy mess Darwin has made of them and work their monstrous depravities while disguised—to my eye, anyhow—as admirable women and men.

Since Darwinian perils may destroy civilization, how is it that Creationist publications in reputable biological journals haven't finally exposed evolution for the anarchical fraud it is? In a word, the answer is "conspiracy." Biologists have globally conspired to back Darwinism and suppress dissent. If you, as a deep thinker on the topic of Intelligent Design, should submit to a legitimate biological journal your scientific paper blowing evolution's cover, the editors, determined to squelch dissent, won't publish it. Nor will other Darwinian editors, because they're all in cahoots.

In the spring of 2008, a company called Premise Media released the Creationist documentary *Expelled,* whose title refers to the alleged suppression of scientific truth by evolutionists. The film is a clumsy flow of cut-and-paste distortions and deceits aimed at discrediting legitimate research. Its crudity alone would be proof positive of Creationism's morally parlous condition, but in Minneapolis that fact grew comically ironic. A respected biologist who is interviewed in the film—though with devious intent—was pulled from among people waiting in line for an April showing of *Expelled* and told not to enter the theater under pain of arrest.

Despite his expulsion from *Expelled,* its cry of "Conspiracy!" continues to play well with Mr. and Mrs. Doe. After all, we Americans are great sympathizers with the underdog, and many of us favor conspiracy theories about UFOs, man on the moon, the John F. Kennedy and Martin Luther King, Jr. assassinations, the HIV epidemic, the 9/11 disaster, the birthplace of President Barack Obama, and so on. Hence, the ID mantra, "teach the controversy," which asks school boards to mandate equal time for Creationist science and evolutionary science. Fair's fair, right?

The fairness gambit is a proven winner, even when the underdog is a Wedge. Okay, since polls show one in two American's doesn't believe Earth goes around the sun, shouldn't we in fairness teach that the solar system is geo-centric? Or at least compromise by teaching that, on some days, Earth goes round the sun and, on other days, the sun goes round planet Earth?

Given the average person's limited knowledge of science, it's unsurprising that the ID strategy for invoking abstruse details of microbiology, coupled with dazzling mathematical "proofs," seems so convincing. How many of us can evaluate fine points in microbiology? Have many of us have a firm mathematical grasp of probability theory? Evolutionary science is by now so biochemically, genetically, and statistically intricate that competent biologists who are not specialists in the field are challenged by its complexity.

Take mathematical probabilities alone. Pseudo-science adores probability stats, owing to the available wealth of fudge factors. Michael Behe—the Copernicus, Newton, and Einstein of Irreducible Complexity—finds the mathematical odds against certain biological mechanisms evolving *naturally* to be so improbable as to absolutely require a Designer.[21] Must it? Two centuries ago, the German poet and amateur scientist Johann Wolfgang von Goethe (1749–1832) dryly reminded his fellows of a fact I cited earlier: "Not every mystery is a miracle."

"Furthermore," say evolution's scientists, "design's obvious omnipresence in nature is one thing, whereas a Designer is a very different thing." Then there's the little matter of dealing from an honest deck and running the numbers. Turns out the commonest occurrences of daily life are also highly improbable.

In his book, *Innumeracy: Mathematical Illiteracy and its Consequences* (1988), Allen Paulos deplores the public's inability to see through dubious assertions which cite big figures. One of his examples gives the odds against getting a particular bridge hand of thirteen cards as 600 billion to one. Further, he points out that, in a well-shuffled deck of fifty-two cards, the odds against any possible sequence are nearly one in ten to the sixty-eighth power. A one followed by sixty-eight zeros goes way beyond astronomical. Does the sequence of each shuffled deck require an Intelligent Designer?

Aside from its assertion of biblical inerrancy, Creationism's sole argument against evolution amounts to saying: "Any effect in the natural world which seems either extremely improbable or is not yet completely understood must have been caused by God." In a famous instance, Sir Isaac Newton (1642–1727) agreed. His theory of gravity, brilliant as it was, left unexplained the complex problem of how the orbiting planets of our solar system stay in equilibrium. Baffled, Newton's intense religiosity led him to declare that divine intervention must account for it. As he wrote in his treatise on optics, "Such a wonderful uniformity in the planetary system, must be the effect of providence."[22] And that was that.

But it wasn't. Nearly a century passed before the French genius Pierre-Simon (1749–1827), marquis de Laplace, worked out the mathematical solution, thus demoting Newton's God hypothesis to the status of a cultural curiosity. Yet no less a person than Napoleon Bonaparte (1769–1821), after perusing Laplace's five-volume work, *Traité de la mécanique céleste* (1798–1827), said to him, "You have written this huge work on the system of the world without once mentioning the author of the universe," whereupon Laplace is reputed to have replied, "Sire, I have no need of that hypothesis."[23] (In the remark, if authentic, "that hypothesis" may not have referred to deity but to a Newtonian formula.) In any case, Pierre-Simon's mathematics proved planetary equilibrium, lunar variation, and other celestial effects to have natural causes. As it happens, the entire history of science amounts to just that sort of advance, taking one by one the spooks out of nature.

Finally and most importantly, Creationism gives Jenny and John Doe what we often long for: the world's bewildering complexity made simpler by far than its realities allow. To satisfy that wish, visitors cram the tiny Creation Evidence Museum in Glen Rose, Texas, just as they flock to the 60,000-square-foot Creation Museum in Petersburg, Kentucky, ten minutes from the Cincinnati International Airport. The $25 million museum offers displays and dioramas inculcating the usual Creationist darkness. A museum explaining Tooth-Fairy Science would have equal validity.[24]

Moving in the opposite direction, something called the Clergy Letter Project has rebuked the anti-Darwinists with a manifesto signed by more than 11,000 Christian clergy anxious to put distance between quack science and themselves. In it they call evolution "a foundational scientific truth . . . upon which much of human knowledge and achievement rests." The letter goes on to deplore Creationism's willful foisting "scientific ignorance" onto our children. To further their cause, many of these signatories have even introduced a church event called "Evolution Sunday," aimed at better informing the faithful on the scientific consensus.[25]

After U.S. District Judge Jones's 2005 ruling in the *Kitzmiller vs. Dover* case cited in an earlier chapter, one might have expected that ID would lose momentum and slow to a whimpering standstill. Not at all. A few years later, the state of Texas appointed Don McLeroy, a believer in ID, to chair the Texas State Board of Education. Only in 2009 did the Texas Senate vote not to confirm him as chair, though he remains a member of the board. Anti-evolution agitation openly continues in Florida, Kansas, Louisiana, Missouri, and New Mexico, among other states. As recently as 2009, the Iowa House of Representatives was asked to consider the implicitly anti-Darwinian "Evolution Education Freedom Act." Happily, it died in committee. But Creationist leaders continue to devise ways and wordings which circumvent the precedent established by the Dover decision. Nor has local intimidation ceased to influence the teaching of science. So the beat does go on.

For Binford Pyle, it all begins with Scripture, to which I now turn my attention.

GOD UPGRADE

Tantum religio potuit suadere malorum.
—Lucretius, *De Rerum Natura*, (I 110)[1]

SURELY, FEW EDUCATED readers believe that a being capable of creating this vast and inexhaustibly astonishing universe is capable of reacting so vengefully as the Old Testament often depicts God. To admit that human projection is the true origin of Yahweh and His mood swings would, however, contradict the fundamentalist doctrine of divine inspiration and biblical inerrancy, so any such a concession becomes, for scriptural literalists, unthinkable.[2]

Roots of that denial go back into the deep past, but as recently as 1978 a manifesto signed by nearly 300 evangelical scholars, the *Chicago Statement on Biblical Inerrancy*, declared "Holy Scripture . . . is to be believed, as God's instruction, in all that it affirms; obeyed, as God's command, in all that it requires. . . ." Furthermore, the statement denies the legitimacy of "any treatment of the text . . . that leads to relativizing . . . or discounting its teaching. . . ."[3] Note the two uses of "all," especially in "all that it affirms."

That "all" is why, as noted in my earlier chapter, "Not So Great Debate," Binford

Pyle's harping on the *Bible*'s absolute moral authority so puzzled me. No objective perusal of the Old Testament could possibly arrive at such a conclusion. Rather than a monolith, the *Bible* is a virtual library of texts written in widely different times by different authors and under very different historical, social, and political influences, not to forget various translations and editions over long periods of time. These decidedly human origins account for many of the *Bible*'s divine mandates, which no sensible person would obey.

Ironically, therefore, Pyle and every fundamentalist claiming that the *Bible*'s authority to be absolute must necessarily do lots of "relativizing" and "discounting." That is, they *must* choose to ignore certain Scriptural injunctions, and ignore them they do by practicing the moral relativism, which they unceasingly and strenuously claim to be the most socially destructive consequence of "Darwin's Deadly Legacy."

The fact that, today, it is criminal to obey numerous biblical injunctions does not, of course, invalidate the *Bible*'s worth as a virtual library of precious historical and cultural documents, many of which embody timeless wisdom and literary excellence. And my intent here is not to rant against religion. Yet the necessity of choosing which of the *Bible*'s decrees to follow and which to reject implicitly admits to the *Bible*'s human origin in specific historical eras and social and political conditions which no longer obtain.

Take the biblical God's narcissism. Only our human nature can explain God's insatiable appetite for flattery. And, if human adulation flags, the Old Testament God, being of human manufacture, doesn't shy from self-praise. Boasting His awesome prowess, His glorious works, and how He can lick all the other gods, this Scriptural God revels in Himself like one of TV's professional wrestlers. His Almightiness could even drown us like rats, as He did everyone not aboard Noah's ark. Adults, children, animals, and all. Or, as He is quick to point out, He could squish us like bugs if He wanted. From the singing of Psalm 109 alone, I learn that He will "cut off the memory of them from the earth" (109:15) and "slay the broken in heart" (109:16). Further, "Let mine adversaries be clothed with shame, and let them cover themselves with their own confusion, as with a mantle" (109:29).

Clearly, the *Bible*'s ancient authors had been, at some historical juncture, greatly impressed by one or another tyrant's absolute power, answerable to no one. Not only did such power seem awesome, but it seemed highly desirable. So, for that matter, does praise. Our human craving for it, falsely projected onto God, has even made centuries of Catholic monks to roll out of bed in the middle of the night to chant how glorious God is. The monks themselves, of course, seek to be praiseworthy by praising, as is, perhaps, true of more than a few churchgoers today. But back to inerrancy.

To understand in what manner today's evangelical fundamentalists implicitly admit that the *Chicago Statement*'s injunction against "relativizing" and "discounting" is an untenable doctrine, we have only to imagine her or his personal response in certain biblical situations. Let's suppose, for example, that the twenty-five-year-old son of our imaginary Creationist comes home to announce his elopement with and marriage to, a devout Muslim woman of the same age. What's more, having studied the *Qur'ân*, he declares that he has turned Muslim himself.

In the Book of Deuteronomy, the Israelites are commanded to kill by stoning anyone who says, "Let us go after other gods, which thou hast not known, and let us serve them" (13:2). Even if the guilty person is your sister, brother, son, daughter, or wife, you must heave the first stone. If this should happen in a city God has provided, all inhabitants—repeat, *all*—must be put to the sword along with their cattle. Their possessions must be burnt and the city forever destroyed. It's right there in the Good Book (Deuteronomy 13:6–16). With his son about to wed a Muslim, will our hypothetical Creationist heave the first stone?

Of course not. His refusal to do so will tacitly admit that to obey the *Bible* in such a case would be bloody murder. *Even more importantly, it will admit that his personal sense of right and wrong must take precedence over Scripture.* Consciously, he will admit no such thing, perhaps not even to himself. Instead, he will do what such believers always do when confronted with an embarrassing passage in Scripture: explain it away. This mandated stoning in Deuteronomy is but an instance among numerous others of human authors attributing a shameful neediness to the divine being they worship.

I remember Sister Mary Denise telling us sixth-graders that some theologians think only round-the-clock prayers ascending from monasteries and convents have kept God from long ago destroying the entire world for its wickedness. (The world God Himself designed.) Considering such sociopathic human tendencies, why had such a God made the world? What did He want with this one? Publicity? Kickbacks?

Besides, shouldn't any and all desires have been pre-satisfied by His perfection? How can a perfectly Perfect Being *want?* Or want to create anything? Doesn't wanting a thing mean you don't have it? Then, too, how could a perfect Creator have regrets? Yet, in Genesis 6:6–7, God is so sorry He made people that He plans to drown the lot. A change of heart has God grudgingly agree to spare a few for a re-seeding program. Thus, He orders Noah to go nautical and build that famous ark.

Small wonder, then, that, as an adolescent, I should grow unconsciously resentful of this choleric God, not realizing how entirely His unamiable behavior derived from human littleness. That resentment, plus my years of being threatened by the biblical deity of radio preachers and televangelists, began to get to me. "Somebody should tell them," I thought, "that this divine egomaniac they praise to the skies needs more than just tweaking."

Take, for example, the biblical God's jealous streak. Absolutely green-eyed with it. But if God is so All-Everything, why the hissy fits about other gods? Low self-esteem? Hardly. Had He thought the cosmos not roomy enough for rivals?

If a creator of this endlessly intricate universe did exist, such a being could sue us for libel. But there I go, projecting onto Her, Him, or It the very human pettiness which a magnanimous divinity couldn't possibly feel, much less stoop to acting on.

Projecting indeed. Doubtless that's also why our troublesome species equipped God with attributes we ourselves crave and only those. Although we'd be too wise and kindly to use it, wouldn't we just love having the righteous power to squish anyone who ticks us off? My debate opponent Binford Pyle equated Darwinians with Hitler, while ignoring the fact that *Der Führer* could have copied the Holocaust straight from bad behavior projected onto the Old Testament divinity.

Yet this Scriptural God has gone nearly 2,000 years since biblical chapters were first written without an upgrade; more than 3,000 years, if you count all the way back to Moses. A deity-recall program is long overdue. And who better to remedy God's defective design if not the designers? A heavy-handed job it was, with our fingerprints all over it. Lest readers unfamiliar with scripture think me guilty of wild exaggeration, I must cite a few instances.

To list more than a few examples of such a God's dumping calamity onto the wicked and innocent together would depress anyone, so a quick sampling will have to do. Indiscriminately killing the first-born of all Egypt, whether human or animal, infant or elder, and letting the Israelites then despoil the Egyptians, would today be considered crimes against humanity (Exodus 12:29–36). God's jealousy of the Midianite deity leads him to deter intermarriage between them and Israelites by visiting upon the latter a plague that kills off 24,000 of His chosen people (Numbers 25:5–9). Not good enough. Too many Midianites left alive. Through connivance with Gideon, God then oversees the battlefield slaughter of 120,000 more Midianites, which results in their eventual extermination (Judges 7 and 8:1–10). Not only was God jealous of the Midianite god, but He arranges their battlefield slaughter so as to lesson Israelite glory and heighten His own role in the carnage (Judges 7:2–7). Still not enough. From Numbers 31:7–18 we learn that, after the Israelites have slain all the Midianite males in battle and captured their women and children, Moses commands them to slay all the male children along with Midianite women not virgins. The victors may then keep those virgins for their own uses. You can only imagine.

Then there's God's genocide of the Amalekites, which Old Testament authors relished so thoroughly they offered three separate versions. Lest Saul shrink from killing Amalekite infants not yet weaned, God forbids any such compunction: "Now go and smite Amalek, and utterly destroy all that they have, and spare them not; but slay both man and woman, infant and *suckling* [emphasis mine], ox and sheep, camel and ass" (1 Samuel 15:3–4). When not ordering breast-feeding babes put to the sword, this mockery God expresses His displeasure through other lethal modes. In 2 Samuel 24:11–15, He offers David a choice of punishments: a three-year famine, a three-month retreat before David's enemies, or three days of pestilence. David chooses the shorter of the afflictions. Then a God-sent pestilence kills 70,000 men.

So much for big figures. The Lord condones intimately familial depravities as well. The great warrior Jephthah, for instance, promises to honor God with human sacrifice, provided the Lord deliver the Ammonites into his hands. Jephthah vows that he will sacrificially slay whomever should first come forth to his house to greet his victorious return from mowing down Ammonites. That wholly innocent person turns out to be his own daughter. Dismayed but undeterred, Jephthah fulfills his vow with no Scriptural hint of divine displeasure (Judges 11:30–40). Despite my critique of Creationist mendacity, I have no doubt that, if asked to butcher newborn babes, all but the most fanatic supporters of that persuasion would follow their own sanity and refuse.

Or take another instance. Imagine your former roommate in college phones to ask your help at a ritual involving his only son. God has spoken to him, demanding he prove his loyalty by offering the lad in sacrifice. This roommate says he, therefore, urgently needs your bricklaying skill in building the altar on which he will slit his son's throat, then make a burnt offering of the boy.

Clearly, your old friend is delusional. He may have heard a voice, but it can't have been that of a true deity worthy the name. So, instead of your showing up with a trowel and mason's level, you're going to bring a psychotherapist and two of your friend's biggest, strongest buddies. But what would a *Bible*-thumping Creationist do? Would he say to himself, "God has spoken, so I must help build the altar"? Of course not. Even while recalling the biblical precedent, he, too, would question his friend's mental health, aware that such no such horrific demand could have could come from a divine source.

True, in the biblical version (Genesis 22), just as Abraham prepares to draw the knife across Isaac's innocent throat, God sends an angel to say, and I paraphrase, "Hold it, Abraham; God was only testing you!" But that last-minute reprieve in no way redeems the episode of its reprehensible nature. Nor does the biblical deity, in letting Satan make trial of Job's fidelity, feel very warm and wonderful either. Instead

HOW IT IS: THE REAL SURREAL

"WHEN I WAS A CHILD," wrote St. Paul (1 Corinthians 13:11), "I spoke like a child, I understood as a child, I thought as a child: but when I became a man, I put away childish ways."

So true. As a child I was the handiwork of God. Was even made in that deity's image and—along with everybody else—was the be all and end all of creation. How much more important can you get? Yet no sooner had I grown up than my status plummeted to that of just another nano speck adrift in a wilderness of stars—because of my fall into knowledge. When Adam and Eve fell, at least God and His fiery-sword wielding angels hung around ever after.

But not for willful ones like me. Thus I had to watch nine flavors of angel, the entire floral-scented bouquet of blessed saints, the world-mothering Madonna, and heaven's trio of deities slowly melt from suitably pastel-colored cloud to the black of interstellar void. So much for Sky City. Unlike one mistakenly disillusioned young Englishman, however, I didn't reel from ale shop to ale shop claiming Darwin's *On the Origin of Species* had destroyed my life. Still, when the center of your world drops out . . . well, that does take some adjusting.

Yet it wasn't Darwin who had filled my trusting little head with religion's celestial apparatus and double-entry accounting. Nor had evolution spurred my with-drawal from Plato's cave into the wonderfully intriguing mystery of what is.

After the Almighty evaporated on me, I must admit that—human ills aside—nature and the universe itself began to seem far more interesting than some All-Everything supernatural. Without a presiding deity, the world's origin and *raison d'être*, if any, became—and remains—my number-one fascination: the unknowable depth and breadth of all we belong to. Even my neutrino-size unimportance within it acquired the freaky grandeur of being that radically dwarfed by its unknowable extent.

In short, if you love living in a mystery as I do, alive is the place to be.

As for living large in nature, the most spacious way is to realize we inhabit a cosmos where change is the sole mode of being, where stasis is impossible, and where nothing in existence ever has or ever can hold still. With all things in motion and the entire universe evolving, religious insistence on the fixity of species over evolutionary flow grows more backward by the day.[1]

Our imperceptible velocities are such that we're never in the same place from one nanosecond to the next.[2] I say "never in the same place" not only because of Earth's diurnal turning and orbital speed. At my northern Colorado latitude, I'm going about 800 miles per hour (m.p.h.). Simultaneously, as Earth carries us all streaking round the sun, that velocity increases by something like 67,000 m.p.h.—which is slow as Antarctic molasses compared to the additional speeds.

Even "drifting," as astronomers so quaintly put it, *within* the Orion arm of the Milky Way, our entire solar system speeds along at 43,000 m.p.h. . Our fairly outward position in the galaxy as it gyres round its own center adds another half-million m.p.h. of hyper-hurtle. But the Milky Way isn't just revolving on its own axis. It's also madly charging elsewhere along with a mob of galaxies in their multi-thousands—separate whirlpools of nuclear fusion whose number astronomers refer to, again in their quaint way, as the Local Group. So there's a whole lot of whizzing going on but where to? Nobody knows. Whatever mega-mass is drawing us thither, it's called—somewhat ominously—the Great Attractor, sucking us and the Local Group toward itself at roughly 1.5 million m.p.h. Our combined m.p.h. amount to a couple of million. And we don't feel a thing.

So what? While our brain's little gray cells rocket along physically, the mind simply can't keep up, nor does any of that warp-speed stuff reach our bodily senses. No matter how many velocities astronomers reel off, our bodies assure us Earth doesn't budge. They remain in sedate denial, as if this were still 5,000 years ago when our planet was the whole world, floating atop the back of a turtle as in some forgotten Emergence myth.

Yes, we're in outer space all right, even while mowing the lawn, a fact widely known but rarely felt. Figuratively speaking, actually *feeling* the truth of it allows you to be out of this world in your own skin. The authors of sacred Scriptures, whether Islamic or Judeo-Christian, knew nothing of such things, as if the natural world existed only insofar as it served human purposes. Intelligent Design's hatred of "Darwinism" arises from a fear that evolution makes nature matter so much it thereby puts God out of a job. Consequently—and irony of all ironies—ID enthusiasts belittle the very deity they claim to honor. But I forget myself. ID's stated aim is to put their Jesus—and no other prince of peace—in public school classrooms.

On our planet alone the queer and quarky phenomena of sub-atomic physics, along with the endlessly adaptative variations in life-forms by the tens of millions, refute by their very number and intricacy the argument for an Intelligent Designer. Instead of contriving such precarious interdependencies as the human body, for example, whose mind-boggling array of them clearly required self-assembly over eons of evolution, a Supreme Intelligence would produce creatures of elegant simplicity, with organs and cellular functions not put together from spare parts. Creationists, therefore, in pushing Irreducible Complexity (IC) as proof of an Intelligent Designer, get things exactly backward. IC tends to suggest the Designer was Rube Goldberg, whereas the only Creator for which we've got irrefragable evidence is Time. If those who can only live in codependency must have an Almighty, you'd think they'd devise one worthy of Creation and our cosmic context.

Through a sequence of exposures totaling nearly twelve days, two specialized cameras on the Hubble Space Telescope combined to achieve images of 10,000 galaxies in a speck of sky just below the Orion constellation. By now those Ultra Deep Field photos have become world-famous. Initially, however, they startled even stargazing professionals. That minuscule bit of black sky one-thousandth the size of a full moon had seemed empty, but the photos showed it a-swarm with galaxies—not just stars, *galaxies*—merging, distorting, dervishing . . . as they appeared shortly after the Big Bang, the original cosmic explosion offered by science to explain the beginning of the known universe. Who, on seeing those galactic frenzies of light as they were a dozen billion years before Earth existed, could help feeling awe? Because my everyday life keeps that perspective in mind, my lower-case sort of creationism reflects it and pervasively.

More than once in this book I've commented on the reciprocal relation between context and one's inner content. Just as knowledge of the cosmos alters who and what we are, who we are alters our context. Not that our awareness of, say, the solar wind, gamma ray bursts, or galactic collisions changes them physically, but that such knowing allows to see each and everything else more fully, which is to say within its fathomable context.

Furthermore, although Edwin Hubble (1889–1953) proved nearly a century ago that the universe is expanding, recent corroborations of that fact reveal that the *rate* of its expansion is accelerating. In altering my physical context, that fact has certainly has altered me, with plenty more to come. During the lifetime of anyone born since 1923, this ever-evolving cosmos has grown beyond our species' ability to absorb the implications.

To a biblical fundamentalist, some of those implications may be strictly forbidden. For example, among cosmologists the multiverse concept has lately risen in hypothetical status. A universe here, another universe there, and so on. Ad *infinitum?* Possibly. But if so, how could its endlessness ever be known? The outer edge of even a finite universe may have already expanded eternally beyond the horizon of observation, toward somewhere no mind can go.

For my own decidedly finite intellect, even the whopping figures which express our cosmic context have become ungraspable digits trailing their zeros like a string of pearls. Though I absolutely love knowing I live in a world queerer than we can ever imagine, can anyone aware of such things avoid feeling slightly problematic? Surely not.

That's why, despite my dim view of fundamentalism and Intelligent Design, I can't help understanding their desperate insistence on a firmly fixed hitching post in this extravagantly wild universe where, literally, every single thing is in motion. Indeed, like Linus's blanket, living in a tight little, right little, firmly closed world is a dubious comfort of a closed mind. Freely espousing an unimaginably vast universe certainly isn't for sissies. Even so, isn't refusal to budge from the shadow world of Plato's cave rather sad?

My fall into knowledge entailed more than the loss of Cloud Nine. It caused cosmic immensity to shrink me to a geometrical point having location but no magnitude. Quite a comedown from once being watched over by angels, by all the saints in heaven, and by a three-person God.

Foregoing my postmortem flight to paradise wasn't nearly so hard to handle as was facing up to a human world in which those who endure unspeakable pain, poverty, squalor, hunger, illness, or crushing injustice can expect no otherworldly redress, ever. Triggered by the terrible helplessness we feel in the presence of great suffering, the impulse to beg divine intervention for those who suffer must be among factors explaining the birth of gods.

We Catholic kids certainly sent a lot of prayers heavenward on behalf of sick parishioners, for China's poor, for India's poor, and for every good outcome under the sun. It felt helpful to believe we were actually doing something. My stint in the military during the Korean War showed me Asia's swarms of famished or pain-stricken people, and acquaintance with the natural world has shown me animals in terrible pain but guilty only of having been born. Like sensation in a long-since amputated limb, my faith-acculturated impulse to beg God's intercession in healing the broken body of a savagely beaten toddler—just one recent instance among innumerable others—hasn't yet entirely given up the ghost or hope.

In short, the so-called problem of evil would be a tough one for believers, if not for organized religion's centuries of practice at explaining away. Even then, major religions must employ SWAT teams of theologians to deal with that one, but for all their glib explaining it never goes away. Life's plights and woes, along with a naive and understandable egoism, are why people insist on an afterlife. Rather than deride such insistence, I find it not only natural, but somewhat endearing, even poignant. For all the bouncy testimonials to what a wonderful blessing life is, we know there's more than enough heartbreak and desolation to go round. A wholly benign world beyond the grave seems little enough to ask. And as with deities, so, too, with afterworlds of bliss: where there's demand, there will be supply.

Nor do I snicker at the believer steering her or his soul toward eternal bliss instead of oblivion. If it were a matter of choice, who on Earth would choose otherwise? What's more, Christianity's offer of "happily ever after" beyond the grave carries a lifetime guarantee.

We heretics, on the other hand, must face a return to the uncolorized nothingness whence we came. By way of coping with that futurity, I remind myself that people never gripe about having floated round in oblivion till birth; nor have I ever heard anyone complain about having gotten a sound night's sleep.

⊹

Undeniably, the cataclysmic randomness of sidereal collisions, black holes, star hatcheries, and supernova explosions going on in the vastitude surrounding us all the time can shade every human enterprise with the gray-scale of futility. "Why write? Why paint or sculpt or dance or sing or write? What's the point?"

As far as that goes, why do anything? Undeniably, the perfect indifference of our universe can be a real downer. No wonder our encoding fights back with various dodges. That's why any life worth living must contain something of great value which it knows isn't there.

Meanwhile, swimming in cosmically deep waters without a life preserver adds more than a touch of adventure to any existence—provided we understand that's where we are and what we're doing. Given the combined mass of inanimate matter in the universe, our merely being alive and aware and neither on fire nor in a black hole . . . is, as noted in an earlier chapter, a highly improbable state.

What's more, if—however briefly—we're among the vanishingly small percent of matter which has consciousness, we may as well pay attention. But consciousness is no life jacket either, and staying afloat in waters unfathomably deep isn't for the faint of heart. As to the point of it all, must there be one? And why lie? Isn't "the point of it all" a synonym for "payday?" Ditto for "meaningful." As if doing your best, lifelong, both to understand where we are and what we are weren't plenty meaningful enough.

Admittedly, there are sad afternoons when nothing works and reality feels too true to be good. As anodyne for watching my loftiest thoughts get downsized to the height of a dust mite, I sometimes welcome even the desperate comfort of Blaise Pascal (1623–1662), the seventeenth-century French writer, scientist, and thinker. He felt himself between what he called "two infinities"—the microscopically small and the astronomically large. Yet he reasoned thus: "Though the universe crush him, man is nobler than the forces that kill him. He understands his mortal nature, whereas the universe knows nothing of it."[3]

Hardly a hip-hip-hooray but quite a cut above thumb-sucking. Yet a modest, astrophysicist's excuse for thinking better of one's self does remain available. Owing to the subtle intricacies of the phenomenon called life, the lowliest living critter among us, even a gnat, is more complex than the day-star, our Sun, that begot it.[4] Factor human intelligence into the comparison and the assertion grows all the truer.

If, however, we put our consciousness to no better use than getting through the day, we've ignored the chance of a lifetime, unmindful that being here and alive is the one strangest thing that can ever happen. Considering the innumerable galaxies overhead and underfoot every living moment, our very ennui is paradoxical. In truth, our may-fly longevity makes boredom a left-handed mercy. It enables the illusion we live a long time. Surrealism? That was just an art category, whereas, rightly seen, each of us is a walking, talking surrealist. Most of the time, consciously or unconsciously, we aren't who we are or where we are.

My own favorite attempts at being where and what I am come in facing sunrises. Just watching the sun's bubble ascend puts me—body and soul—in a cosmos. The duality in everything, however, means that the most gorgeous of dawns doesn't lessen the difference between the sun's longevity and mine, just colors the humdrum of gray matter. That same duality also supplies an awareness that our day-star has only nuclear fusion at heart with an opposite realization: we owe it everything—including my touch of sadness at knowing it, too, is mortal.

Occasionally at sunrise, to get perspective on myself, I swap my stance on the mesa slope near our Boulder house for one on the sun. Afloat on the surface of its photosphere I look back toward Earth's pinprick of shine, not quite swallowed up by the blackness of space, and wish others could share the view.

Not only that. I once briefly believed that, if on some miraculous day we humans fully faced and accepted our actual situation, we'd take better care of our planet and each other. It's still my favorite pipedream that won't happen; but, as the song says, "I Can Dream, Can't I?" So, while standing on the sun and looking toward Earth, I occasionally imagine that my wishful figment may one day be realized. There we'll be, all of us, companionably riding our planet's tiny brightness, holding hands and gazing silently out into the question of questions.

A WAY OF BEING: CALL THAT A RELIGION?

. . . whatsoever things are true, whatsoever things are honest,
whatsoever things are just, whatsoever things are pure,
whatsoever things are lovely, whatsoever things are of good report,
if there be any virtue, and if there be any praise, think on these things.
—St. Paul, Philippians 4:8.

MORE THAN ONCE in the course of these pages I've referred to my essentially religious way of seeing and being. Yet only in writing this book have I fully realized that's what it is. I've, therefore, unwittingly enacted a key point in an earlier chapter, "Ecotone Made of Words," where I talk about writing as a path to discovery.

To the extent that religion can be defined as "an explanation of the world," my lower-case creationism has indeed been, for all its meager results, a religious quest. Oddly enough, I dislike the word "religious." It gives off pretentious vibes. Used of one's self, it sounds like an advertisement. Moreover, instead of connoting what "religion" ought to stand for—openness to the world and reverence for all that's within it—millions of nominally "religious" persons accept creeds with lots of answers and few questions. I prefer the reverse.

Furthermore, my solar maker isn't into commandments, cares not a photon who does or doesn't honor its reappearance, nor cares what I make of its Scriptures. Although my way of seeing has moved from theo-centric to geo-centric, to cosmo-centric, it's nevertheless a worldview increasingly shared around the globe by persons who don't think of their outlook—or, perhaps, of themselves—as religious. Aside from condemning hurtful behavior, our sole moral absolute regards the health of this planet and its citizen life-forms.

Followers of the great religions of the world erect ponderous mosques, synagogues, supras, temples, and cathedrals to give heft and presence to deities conspicuously absent. Many of them offer great rewards to their believers, whereas my way offers only a heightened awareness of the natural world whose echo we are.

Christian orthodoxy, to be sure, promises a far sweeter deal. Twelve-gated city, streets paved with gold (or the equivalent), and everybody loves you, especially God . . . unless you've been more naughty than nice. Compared to an all-loving Father and world-mothering Madonna, my religion isn't nearly so familial and comfy. Furthermore, since I'll not get paid for good behavior, and whatever merit I may have isn't being credited to my account for redeeming on the other side of the grave, my reward must flow from appreciating, even reverencing, the greatly mysterious story of natural phenomena to which we bear witness: evidence of Creation and its evolutionary nature.

As a Coloradan I wasn't surprised that the Baylor University survey, mentioned earlier in "Deity Upgrade," found the deity most favored by believers living in the American West to be the aloof cosmic power of Type D, nor was I startled at its finding more unbelievers in the West than in any other part of the nation.[1] Open country, open mind? That may seem too simplistic, but it also seems true that open country induces in us interrogative moods.

Yesterday, in walking a loop of Boulder's nearby Mesa Trail with my out-of-town friend Denise, we paused over a seep where the pure flax-flower blue of six or seven small butterflies hovered and winked. At full stretch their wingspan wasn't wide as my thumb, a fact easily seen from two motionless ones floating upon, and stuck flat to, an inch-deep pool fed by the seep. Drowned in sipping too close? Denise took one of the sopped victims on her forefinger, and we resumed our walk.

Its wings must have dried quickly. Before we had gone a hundred yards we were treated to a resurrection. Apparently, none the worse for floating face down, it stirred, gave a flutter, then went winking off and away in that jittery zigzag of butterflies.

We rejoiced, of course, because one life is all lives. Darwin and the discovery of DNA elevated that insight to science, but it was felt eons before, and Denise's response to its truth was expressed in her touch. Such an awareness of our ties to all that is—our kinship to it—centers my religion. Pretty simple.

I like simple. No worship, no prayer, and all precepts rolled into one: "Do as little harm as reasonably possible." That's scarcely a maverick stance, inasmuch as the outlook I've called "my religion" is shared by people of all kinds and conditions. What could be less doctrinaire than a slight variant of the ancient Hippocratic prescription for a physician's care of his patient? Finally, no Scriptures other than Sun-written ones. Instead, a way of seeing, of being.

But what of ritual? Well, aside from random acts of careful attention, my sole ritual, as I mentioned in the last chapter, is a penchant for watching the sun come up and even then only when I really feel like it, as, more often than not, I very much do. After all, religions didn't begin as doctrines but as feelings. Codifying and franchising God came later, in the interest of control. The truest creed isn't doctrinal, just a certain vision. Call it an attitude, one permeating daily behavior. In the very word "religion" there may be some warrant for that. Oddly, considering its importance, the word's origin isn't clear. Among etymological surmises, the most likely one relates the Latin *religio* to *religare*, which refers to tying, binding back, or, perhaps, binding together.

Obviously, Creationists, by their denial of kinship with other mammals, illustrate why "going by the Good Book" literally, mindlessly, can be so diminishing. Science, to the extent that it clarifies where and what we are, shares religion's explanatory role while being quite unlike religion in two crucial respects. First, scientific findings undergo endless re-examination, and, second, they're limited to the natural world. Any religion wary of science is wary of knowledge, so it's reasonable to ask, "Why? What are you so afraid of knowing? And which attitude do you think has been more beneficial to the human race: credulity or skepticism?"

Two decades ago, gratefully hurtling along in the astronomically lucky orbit of Earth, I felt the absence, then presence, of life so vividly the moment became indelible. With my backpacking pal Ron I was heading up the trail to Buchanan Pass, which tops out at 11,837 feet on the Continental Divide. Our approach to the foot of Buchanan had been wearisome, trudging up through a half-desolate valley in which much of the side-slope timber had been blown down. Back from two months in Europe, I hadn't done anything more strenuous than a couple of day-hikes in Italy's Dolomites, hadn't even re-acclimated to Colorado's altitude, and certainly wasn't in shape for lugging a thirty-five-pound pack. After the tedious six-mile hike to the pass, we still had to walk three further miles beyond, steeply descending, then again climbing to Gourd Lake.

Ron and I usually kept to the same pace. Together we've spent many a gorgeous high-country day that couldn't have held more, but, like any male, I'd rather risk a coronary than say, "Hey, I'm tired," especially if the other fellow isn't. But not this time. Once we'd begun ascending to the pass, my body winced with each step, my pack felt like a gravity sponge, and my spirits were about as lively as the bleakly gray, cinder-fine scree right and left of me on that east side of the Divide.

There wasn't a bush nor one blade of grass to be seen. No green whatever. Not even lichen. Flanked by rock and scree drained of color, I felt like turning back. Instead, I found a sittable boulder several times before topping out and admitted I needed a five-minute break.

Going up, Ron had stayed well ahead, then down over the pass and out of sight. When I topped out there I saw his small figure already way below in the valley on the other side. Four days later, however, our return up to Buchanan from the western slope was another story entirely.

Terrain east of the Divide lives in the rain shadow of the Rockies, whereas the western side gets so much more snow and rain as to be lush by comparison. Coming back, our approach to the pass led us, therefore, through a succulent meadow the map calls Fox Park. Instead of passing trees blasted by storm, like those on the eastern side of the pass, we found ourselves among evergreens straight and tall. So we wound, switchbacking, past hearty Douglas-fir and Engelmann spruce rising from greenly luxuriant undergrowth on trunks a yard thick. All about us, all the way, flowers bloomed by the galactic millions. When down lower, we passed marsh marigolds, elephantella, buttercups, and blue bells; then, a bit higher, admired columbine, fireweed, the purple-violet of penstemon, and the intense crimson of Indian paint brush along much of the trail. Flowers galore, by all means.

This time I was doing the leading while it was Ron who fell behind. Later, he said the pace had been much too fast for him, but I wasn't dishing out payback, just feeling so good I couldn't help it. During the days we spent camped at Gourd Lake, rambling around and above it, I had dreaded the slog back up and over the pass. Now, puzzled by my own stamina, my heart fairly sang, even though my forehead was dropping bead after bead of sweat, each falling clear as I leaned into the trail's steepness. Where, I wondered, was my energy coming from? Mushy as it may sound, the only possible answer was flower power.

Life's verve flourished all around me, beginning in those succulent-looking meadows of Fox Park now far below, emerald as Ireland, with me rejoicing in that florabundance of blooms—cerulean blue, sulphur yellow, royal purple, fire wagon red—nodding societies of blossom, their petals in all the colors of hope.

Last week, while watching a documentary about Russian astronauts cooped for weeks in their instrument-crammed space station, I saw a parallel. Every now and then, a crew member would stand for minutes at a time staring into a small glass enclosure whose gro-lites encouraged a tiny plot of wheat, its stems and leaves lushly, exuberantly green.

I knew the feeling. And how. It feels like love.

When, sweat-soaked and shivering in torrential gusts that kept pouring over the Divide, I once again topped out on Buchanan Pass, I fumbled my sky-blue parka out of its stuff-sack and laughed to see big wind whap it open like a flag.

Because most human conceptions of deity barely rise past the juvenile, people often say, "But, if there were no God, life would be meaningless." Always, the words are spoken by a speaker sincerely mistaking opinion for fact and equating "meaningful" with some kind of jackpot or justification.

Meaningless? If you say so. Whenever my emotions have flatlined in that direction, and the dailyness of life has grown wearisome, just recalling our terrestrial/celestial situation invariably perks up my spirits. They may not soar, but they do chirp and flutter a little, reminding me, "So here you are, a talking mammal being hustled through outer space literally faster than a shooting star—to nobody knows where."

Gotta love our strangeness of place.

My sense of that fact has also helped keep me real. Gazing into any pair of eyes, friend's or total stranger's, I may remember to see behind brown, blue, or green irises the long journey through evolutionary time to right now. It's then I feel the pathos of our brevity. Eyes understood geo-temporally give me a warmer sense of kinship than—to my considerable surprise—the greatest of world literature, much as I love it. The reason? Simple as mortals looking into each other and seeing themselves. Even disagreeable people grow a bit easier to take if looked at that way. Their vision is poor. They can't see our situation, don't know what and where they are.

Aside from fellow feeling, therefore, the best worldview we mortals can have is one affording some sense of the Big Picture, starting with Creation. As implied throughout this book, that's pretty much coextensive with my kind of creationism, my kind of religion.

An aspect I particularly enjoy comes of realizing that nobody on Earth knows what lies outside the frame or if there is one. Consequently, if where you are alters what you are—as indeed it does—we and what Robert Frost called "the whole she-bang" are in an ultimate sense unknowable, for ever and ever, amen. Somehow, far from inducing despair, that feels intriguing enough to be a promotion.

To live in a world that wasn't meant, just is, doesn't make native grasses, starry nights, tanagers, mountain torrents, forests, badgers, magpies, or honey bees any more meaningless than do absentee deities. One finch perching a thistle becomes rather fascinating when contextualized by the solar system and beyond. So does the thistle. Sadly, if we're blind to time's cunning in things miniscule or enormous, what we look on is meager compared to what's there.

Till one of those deities painted on the ceiling has the gumption to make a personal appearance and start atoning, the meaning of life must be our contented or joyous awareness of being alive—even if the source of that meaning is us and of the rainbow's gold as well.

Some twenty years ago, the deepest glimpse I've ever had into whatever this is that we're a part of came about while backcountry skiing. In Medieval times and later, it would have been thought a vision and a mystical one at that. Yet I'm a decidedly un-visionary person, skeptical all over the place. Nevertheless, what I saw—and felt with once-in-a-lifetime intensity—while skiing on a wind-frigid February afternoon in Glacier Gorge still feels, after all those years, the truest moment I've ever lived.

Under a sky whose high-altitude blue deepened toward purple when I looked straight overhead, it had been an exciting but bitterly cold afternoon of wildly blowing snow. Nonetheless, I kept warm by pouring out energy as, on skis, I ascended Glacier Gorge, a U-shaped valley gouged out during the last Ice Age, and all the while being overlooked by iron peaks several thousand feet higher, right, left, and up ahead.

Already at the trailhead it had been snowing sideways. For hours thereafter my upward gliding got intermittently whelmed by locally cyclonic whirls of snow, forcing me to a standstill, eyes tightly shut, with each manic vortex making me fight for my breath. Repeatedly all afternoon, I also paused to watch, from between wet lashes, high torrents of snow spuming off summits. Two and three air-miles distant, their whirling crystals leapt soundlessly up off the peaks like dervishes flying fast away.

Those cold and windy swirls down below made tightening laces on my ski boots a painful process. Though my feet never go numb, my hands are a problem. To doff ski mittens for more than fifteen seconds risked frostbitten fingers, which meant working at each boot only briefly before thrusting my icy hands into the pockets of my wool knickers. Once circulation was restored, they ventured out again for another quick go. But wind chill sucked away their warmth so fast that just snugging those laces took between ten and twelve minutes.

On reaching Black Lake, some five miles up the gorge and surrounded on three sides by cliffs partly glazed with great plates of ice looking a milky blue-green, I skied even higher to a mile-wide glacial bowl above the ice lake, where the austerity of blue snow and silvered stone on peaks all around me became the reward I was reluctant to leave. Although I wanted to glide around a while, enjoying what my energy had earned, the reddening winter sun was already sinking toward high ridgelines to the west. Descent to the trailhead would go a lot faster than the ascent, but it seemed best to begin heading back. In wilderness, especially alone, it's wise to allow yourself some leeway, some margin, whether of time, food, extra clothing, or, in this case, of daylight.

To my left the lowering sun tinted wrecked hulks of snow-streaked granite, while above them twelve-storey spicules and Colosseum-size flakes seemed about to say something important. But, no, they were just so much cold stone.

Then, looking way back and above the Glacier Gorge headwall of mountains from which the wind-ripped snow had kept streaming pell mell, I was transfixed. Held by the slow wheel of one vast and luminous gyre, I stood staring at it for some time, puzzled; then understood what I was seeing: All that is. The one true thing. Felt not as a deity but a power worlds beyond my own little whiff of existence and these pitiful schemes we believe we believe in.

So there I stood, spellbound by more than just snow ripped from escarpments of granite. Within the slow wheel of its immense incandescence I was seeing myself both alive and long gone, shot with my own blood. I knew that radiant power was bound to annihilate me and all it makes, as it must, to be what it is. For the first time in my life I felt myself hopelessly, inescapably, mortal.

And, though I've never been so terrified, I couldn't wish that presence, that power, other than it was. Couldn't both see it and want to do that. Could only say "yes" and accept my own extinction as part of what must be, to be as it should.

Then its awesome brilliance waned to something tremendously gone, and I realized even our ingenious planet is, by comparison, as brief as a blown snowflake.

Returned to myself, I was back in a steep glacial valley. Many thousands of feet higher, the summit of Longs Peak warmed itself at the last of sundown, then softened to alpenglow fast losing color—as if the life of that long afternoon were slowly turning to stone. I watched till the final rays went dull and the last of the sun's red gold got sucked into granite.

Then stood there a few moments more, in sympathy with the great-hearted, snow-laden fir, the hugely stupid boulders I love, the dear wind-haggard spruce, the wind-flustered ravens. All of us, one sky-lit and empty blue.

For early risers, dawn offers an up-close and personal way of living large, which makes that time of day my favorite. A gift. Usually, I stand on the slope of an alluvial mesa left by an inland sea, which withdrew more than sixty million years ago. Right and left of me lounge red boulders whose age makes ancient Egypt seem lately. Waiting for the sun's bubble to rise from our Colorado plain, I'm an evolved mammal thinking in one of Earth's recent languages. Then, as I described earlier, for an even truer perspective I imagine standing on the sun and looking back at Earth's dim glint amid interstellar blackness.

As a matter of fact, our day-star's planetary encore drew me out again this spring morning. I listened, heard feathered voices taking it from the top. Meadowlarks? Yes, they, April's own—whose clear song ran fresh variations on how to live, what to do about daybreak. Old as call and reply their trills floated to and fro from atop a yucca stalk or squawbush twig with the lilt of an answerable future. "How to live," they said, "is to be here completely." And what do? "Sing for your territory or die."

Oh, I know. On our planet full of hot magma, lark notes to dawn aren't meant, they're encoded, but I thought about that and about the sun's molten gold received as mere physics.

A slight breeze flowed over grasses all down the mesa, setting seed-heavy tassels on stems to sinking, then rising, then sinking again. A raven pair flapped past and away, floating apart, then closing the distance between them in those graceful veers and glides which mated ravens all use. Into three cottonwoods at the foot of the slope fluffed several of my raucous familiars, the magpies. Slowly, the line of our eastern horizon brightened, then burst open—as the rim of the solar sphere flooded the eyes with dazzle.

Given my almost daily attendance at dawn's punctual mirage, just what, I asked myself, am I half-hoping to sense? Some hint of my life's farthest cause and true nature? Maybe so, even though its mystery is knowable only as forever what happens. Yet, facing the brilliantly seminal power of nuclear fusion, song rises inwardly anyway . . . at this latest return of the fire that first made us human.

NOTES

Note to the Reader: Because *Living Large in Nature* is not an academic treatise, I have fully documented only those statements and sources I deem most relevant to the connection between Darwinian and anti-Darwinian perspectives. Also, my translation of Virgil, in the epigraph on page vii, is: "Happy is he [she] who can know the causes of things."

Prologue

1. Credit for natural selection and evolution should equally be given to Darwin's contemporary, Alfred Russel Wallace (1823–1913). See Jane Camerini, editor, *The Alfred Russel Wallace Reader: A Selection of Writings from the Field,* with a foreword by David Quammen (Baltimore: The Johns Hopkins University Press, in association with the Center for American Places, 2002).

2. From 1982 to the present, Gallup has been polling on human origins. In that time, between forty-three percent and forty-seven percent of those questioned held the following opinion: "God created human beings pretty much in their present form at one time within the last 10,000 years or so." See http://www.gallup.com/poll/108226/republicans-democrats-differ-creationsim.aspx. In a British Council poll of 2009, forty-six percent of U.S. respondents felt it impossible to believe in God and evolution.

A Challenge

1. *Science,* No. 313 (2006): 765–66.

2. Keith Graham, Delores Shimmin, and George Parker Thompson, *Biology: God's Living Creation,* 2nd ed. (Pensacola, FL: Beka Books, 1999). Available online at www.pandasthumb.org/archives/2007/05/acsi-v-stearns.html.

3. www.cosmosmagazine.com/news/367/world-science-academics-hit-back.

4. Fourth edition, published by Benziger Brothers, Inc., 1952, and reprinted by the Seraphim Company, Inc., Colorado Springs, 2001.

5. Ibid., 33.

6. Hereinafter I refer to *The Holy Bible* as the *Bible.*

7. Op. cit., 37.

Ecotone Made of Words

1. My translation is: "The secret aim of an artist is to make himself other and more than he is . . . through his work.

2. Cited by Arthur Peacocke, "The Challenge and Stimulus of the Epic of Evolution to Theology," in Steven J. Dick, ed., *Many Worlds: The New Universe, Extraterrestrial Life, and the Theological Implications* (Philadelphia and London: Templeton Foundation Press, 2000), 109.

3. The Dillard remark was reported to me by another writer who, like me, was a speaker at an arts festival held every spring by Ohio University.

4. Reported to me in a conversation with Rexroth himself.

Not So Great Debate

1. The citation is from "A Designer Universe" in Steven Heinberg, *Facing Up: Science and Its Cultural Adversaries* (Cambridge: Harvard University Press, 2001), 231.

2. Cited in John Bartlett, *Familiar Quotations,* 16th ed. (Boston: Little, Brown and Company, 1992), 271.

3. Eric Harris and Dylan Klebold were the two responsible for the Columbine

slaughter, the one a born psychopath, the other seriously depressed. See Dave Cullen, *Columbine* (New York: Twelve, 2009), *passim.*

4. The catch phrase "survival of the fittest" originated with Herbert Spencer (1820–1903), a contemporary of Darwin, who then borrowed it ill-advisedly, according to Arthur Peacocke (b. 1924), a scientist and Anglican priest.

5. On 5 August 2007, I listened to D. James Kennedy recite, in a nationally televised address, the same mendacities voiced by Binford Pyle in his calumny of Darwin and evolution.

Deities on the Ceiling and the Theology of Up

1. See Robert Lenoble, *La géologie au milieu du XVII siècle,* "Les Conférences du Palais de la Découverte," Série D, No. 27 (Paris, France: Université de Paris, 1954), 3–4.

2. My translation is from the essay, "Les Météores," in *Oeuvres de Descartes: Discours del la Méthod & Essais* (Paris, France: Librairie Philosophique J. Vrin, 1965), 231.

3. This and all subsequent biblical passages presented in this book come from the authoritative and now rare edition, *The Holy Bible: Authorized or King James Version Containing the Old and New Testaments Translated out of the Original Tongues and with the Former Translations Diligently Compared and Revised* (Philadelphia: Universal Book and Bible House, n.d.).

William Paley's Very Wonderful Watch

1. According to a memoir written by his disciple and biographer, Xenophon, no less a person than Socrates chose the eye to illustrate the Argument from Design. In Xenophon's *Memorabilia* (1.4.6), he is quoted as doing so in detail. I have used the Boston edition of Paley's work, published by Gould and Lincoln, 1855.

2. See, for example, John Allen Paulos, *Irreligion: A Mathematician Explains Why the Arguments of God Just Don't Add Up* (New York: Hill and Wang, 1980). And see my later chapter, "Pinocchio's Nose."

3. *The Nature of the Gods,* trans. by P. G. Walsh (Oxford, UK: Clarendon Press, 1997), 80–81.

4. Ibid.

5. As quoted in Anthony Kenny, *Ancient Philosophy,* Vol. I (Oxford, UK: Clarendon Press, 2004), 290.

6. Angelo Pasquinelli, ed., *I Presocratici: Frammenti e testimonianze,* I (Torino, Italy: Giulio Einaudi, 1958), 248.

7. Ibid.

The Darwinian Divinity Called Time

1. A similar poll taken in Canada online in July 2008 reported only twenty-two percent favoring the all-God and "10,000 years ago" alternative.

2. Earth's age is estimated at about 4.5 or 4.6 billion; the origin of life began some 3.5 billion years ago.

3. See www.pollingreport.com/science.htm.

Adam's Needful Navel

1. See Martin J. S. Rudwick, *Bursting the Limits of Time: The Reconstruction of Geohistory in the Age of Revolution* (Chicago: The University of Chicago Press, 2005).

2. Sir Archibald Geikie, *Landscape in History and Other Essays* (New York: Macmillan and Co., 1905), 183. The words cited appear in an essay of 1882.

3. Adrian Desmond and James Moore, *Darwin* (New York: Warner Books, 1991), xviii.

4. Edmund Gosse, *Father and Son: A Study of Two Temperaments* (London, UK: William Heinemann Ltd, Windmill Library Edition, 1928), 105.

5. Ibid., 1.

6. Ibid., 105.

7. Ibid., 108.

The Geo-Theology of Down

1. A. Hallam, *Great Geological Controversies* (Oxford, UK: Oxford University Press, 1983), vii.

2. Gertrude Himmelfarb, *Darwin and the Darwinian Revolution* (New York: W. W. Norton, 1962), 239.

3. Edward B. Bailey, *James Hutton–the founder of Modern Geology* (London, UK: Elsevier Publishing, 1967), 65.

4. Archibald Geikie, *Landscape in History and Other Essays* (New York: MacMillan and Company, 1905), 200–01, citing Hutton's *Theory of the Earth,* Vol. I, 173.

Arias and Atom Bombs

1. Denise Royal, *The Story of Robert Oppenheimer* (London, UK: St. Martin's Press, 1969), 49.

2. Emilio Segrè, *Enrico Fermi, Physicist* (Chicago: The University of Chicago Press, 1970), 133–34.

3. Bernice Brode, *Tales of Los Alamos* (Los Alamos, NM: LASL Community News, 1960), June 2 and September 22: ix and 7, respectively.

4. Laura Fermi, *Atoms in the Family* (Chicago: The University of Chicago Press), 60.

5. Alice Kimball Smith and Charles Weiner, eds., *Robert Oppenheimer: Letters and Recollections* (Cambridge: Harvard University Press, 1980), 10.

6. Ibid., 70.

7. Richard Rhodes, *The Making of the Atomic Bomb* (New York: Simon & Schuster, 1988), 664.

Journey to the Center Place

1. T. S. Eliot, *Collected Poems 1909–1962* (New York: Harcourt, Brace & World, 1963), 176.

Pinocchio's Nose

1. As quoted in "Judge Rules Against 'Intelligent Design,'" *The Washington Post* (21 December 2005). The article, as syndicated by the Associated Press and dated 20 December 2005, can be read online at http://www.msnbcmsncom/id/10545387.

2. On *The Origin of Species,* sixth edition of the 1876 publication, in Paul H. Barrett and R. B. Freeman, eds., *The Works of Charles Darwin,* Vol. 16 (New York: New York University Press, 1988), 421.

3. From the Website: www.nabt.org/sub/positionstatements/evolution.asp. As an interesting point of information, Professor Jane Bock informs me that the cited words are those of the distinguished geneticist Theodosius Dobzhansky (1900–1975), an orthodox Christian.

4. John Allen Paolos, *Irreligion: A Mathematician Explains Why the Arguments for God Just Don't Add Up* (New York: Hill and Wang, 2008), 19.

5. As quoted in Barbara Forrest and Paul R. Gross, *Creationism's Trojan Horse: The Wedge of Intelligent Design* (Oxford, UK: Oxford University Press, 2004), 215.

6. Ibid., 158.

7. Cited in John Bartlett, *Familiar Quotations,* 16th ed. (Boston: Little Brown and Company, 1992), 603.

8. www.arn.org/wedge.htm.

9. William Dembski, *Intelligent Design: The Bridge Between Science and Theology* (Downers Grove, IL: Inter Varsity, 1999), 206–07.

10. Michael Behe, *Darwin's Black Box: The Biochemical Challenge to Evolution* (New York: Free Press, 1996), 232–33.

11. Dembski, 252.

12. www.pbs.org/wgbh/nova/id/defense-id.html.

13. As quoted in Charles P. Pierce, *Idiot America: How Stupidity Became a Virtue in the Land of the Free* (New York: Doubleday, 2009), 9.

14. Author's conversation with David Stock, University of Colorado, Boulder.

15. "Fighting for our Sanity in Tennessee," an essay first published in *Free Inquiry,* Vol. 34, No. 4 (Fall 2001): 2. Cited from www.etsu.edu/philos/faculty/NIALL/sanity.in.tennessee.htm.

16. www.pjvoice/com/v3/006/frist.html.

17. See http://www.icr.org/article/review-pbs-evolution-series/.

18. Ibid., www.icr.org/tenets, "Principles of Biblical Creationism."

19. Henry Morris, *The Troubled Waters of Evolution* (San Diego: Creation Life, 1974), 74–75.

20. The poll's wording was clear: "The Earth orbits the sun and takes a year to do it. True or False?"

21. Michael Behe, *Darwin's Black Box* (New York: The Free Press, 1996), *passim*.

22. See Derek Gjersten, *The New York Handbook* (London, UK: Routledge and Kegan Paul, 1986), 510–11.

23. Bartlett, 351.

24. See Kenneth Chang, "Paleontology and Creationism Meet but Don't Mesh," *The New York Times* (30 June 2009): D4.

25. www.butler.edu/clergyproject/religion_science_collaboration.htm.

God Upgrade

1. My translation is: "To such heights of wickedness can beliefs persuade." The title of Lucretius's poem means roughly "On Nature."

2. As to God's mood swings, in *The Evolution of God* (New York: Little Brown and Company, 2009), Robert Wright illustrates how changing historical conditions account for God's alternation between rigorous and relaxed attitudes. See, also, Robert Wright's op ed, "A Grand Bargain Over Evolution," *The New York Times* (23 August 2009): WK9.

3. The complete document can be read at www.spurgeon.org/~phil/creeds/chicago.html.

4. That appeal is not without serious repercussions for the health of our planet. U.S. Congressman John Shimkus, of Illinois, at an April 2009 hearing of the Energy and Commerce Committee, refuted the worst-case scenario on global warming by reading aloud a modern translation of God's promise in Genesis 8:21: "Never again will I destroy all living creatures as I have done." He then affirmed his belief that was "the infallible word of God," a view widely shared among fundamentalists.

5. See Bart D. Ehrman, *Misquoting Jesus: The Story Behind Who Changed the Bible and Why* (San Francisco; Harper Collins, 2005).

6. As quoted in *Shaw's Dramatic Criticism (1895–98): A Selection by John F. Matthews* (New York: Hill and Wang, 1959), 45.

7. Available at www.baylor.edu/isreligion/index.

8. Cited in John Bartlett, *Familiar Quotations*, 16th ed. (Boston: Little Brown and Company, 1992), 520.

How It Is: The Real Surreal

1. On 30 June 2009, the British Council's "Darwin Now" program released results of an international survey designed to measure awareness of evolution in ten countries: Argentina, China, Egypt, Great Britain, India, Mexico, Russia, and the U.S. Of the U.S. adults polled, forty-six percent felt it impossible to believe in God and evolution. See www.britishcouncil.org/darwinnow-survey-global.pdf.

2. Roughly, a nanosecond is the amount of time it takes for light to travel twelve inches.

3. The translation is mine and comes from Michel Le Guern, ed., *Oeuvres complètes* (Paris, France: Editions Gallimard, 2000), 614.

4. So says astronomer Martin J. Rees, "Humanity's Place in Cosmic Evolution," in Steven J. Dick, ed., *Many Worlds: The New Universe, Extraterrestrial Life, and the Theological Implications* (Philadelphia and London: Templeton Foundation Press, 2000), 69.

A Way of Being: Call That a Religion?

1. "American Piety in the 21st Century" (September 2006): 29. Available online at www.baylor.edu/isreligion/index.

ABOUT THE AUTHOR

Reg Saner was born in 1931 in the farm town of Jacksonville on the Illinois prairie. He first saw mountains during military service when he was sent to Big Delta, Alaska, for alpine and arctic survival training. After his combat experience as an infantry platoon leader in the Korean War, he studied Renaissance culture at the University of Illinois and as a Fulbright Scholar at the Universitá degli Studi in Florence, Italy. On honeymooning in Colorado, he and his wife, Anne, decided to move there. In 1962, Reg Saner joined the faculty of the University of Colorado in Boulder, where he is a Distinguished Professor of English.

His previous writings have won many national prizes, including the first Walt Whitman Award as conferred by the Academy of American Poets and the Copernicus Society of America; a National Poetry Series "Open Competition" winner, selected by Derek Walcott; a National Endowment for the Arts Creative Writing Fellowship; the Creede Repertory Theater Award; the State of Colorado's Governor's Award for Excellence in the Arts; and the Wallace Stegner Award, conferred by the Center of the American West. In 1999, Saner was named Boulder's first Poet Laureate.

Saner is the author of four books of poetry and three other books of nonfiction: *The Four-Cornered Falcon: Essays on the Interior West and Natural Scene* (The Johns

Hopkins University Press, in association with the Center for American Places, 1993; Kodansha trade paperback, 1994), *Reaching Keet Seel: Ruin's Echo & the Anasazi* (The University of Utah Press, 1998), and *The Dawn Collector: On My Way to the Natural World* (The Center for American Places, 2005). His prose and poetry have appeared in more than 140 magazines, including *The Atlantic, The Georgia Review, The Gettysburg Review, Ohio Review, Orion, The Paris Review, Poetry,* and *The Yale Review,* and in more than fifty anthologies, including *Fifty Years of American Poetry, The Pushcart Anthology,* and *Best American Essays.*

ABOUT THE BOOK

Living Large in Nature: A Writer's Idea of Creationism is the fourth volume in the *Center Books in Natural History* series, George F. Thompson, series founder and director. The book was brought to publication in an edition of 1,000 hardcover copies with the generous financial support of the Friends of the Center for American Places, for which the publisher is most grateful. The text was set in Whitman, the paper is Glatfelter Offset, 60-pound weight, and the book was professionally printed and bound in the United States of America. For more information about the Center for American Places at Columbia College Chicago, please see page 136.

FOR THE CENTER FOR AMERICAN PLACES AT
COLUMBIA COLLEGE CHICAGO:

George F. Thompson, Founder and Director

Charles E. Little, David R. Moyer, and
    Rev. Ed Piper, Special Advisers

Susan Arritt, Consulting Editor

Brandy Savarese, Editorial Director

Jason Stauter, Operations and Marketing Manager

Erin F. Fearing, Executive Assistant

Purna Makaram, Manuscript Editor

Abigail Friedman, Book Designer

David Skolkin, Art Director

Center for American Places
AT COLUMBIA COLLEGE CHICAGO

The Center for American Places at Columbia College Chicago is a nonprofit organization, founded in 1990 by George F. Thompson, whose educational mission is to enhance the public's understanding of, appreciation for, and affection for the places and spaces that surround us; that is, the natural, built, and social landscapes of the world—whether urban, suburban, rural, or wild—with an emphasis on North America. Underpinning this mission is the belief that books provide an indispensable foundation for comprehending and caring for the places where we live, work, and commune. Books live. Books endure. Books make a difference. Books are gifts to civilization.

Since 1990 the Center for American Places at Columbia College Chicago has brought to publication more than 330 books under its own imprint and in association with numerous publishing partners. Center books have won or shared more than 100 editorial awards and citations, including multiple best-book honors in more than thirty fields of study.

For more information, please send inquiries to the Center for American Places at Columbia College Chicago, 600 South Michigan Avenue, Chicago, Illinois 60605–1996, U.S.A., or visit the Center's Website (*www.americanplaces.org*).